VGM Opportunities Series

OPPORTUNITIES IN **SUMMER CAMP CAREERS**

Blythe Camenson

Foreword by
Connie Coutellier
Director Professional Development
American Camping Association

VGM Career Horizons
NTC/Contemporary Publishing Company

Library of Congress Cataloging-in-Publication Data

Camenson, Blythe
    Opportunities in summer camp careers/Blythe Camenson.
        p. cm. – (VGM opportunities series)
    ISBN 0-8442-2344-1 (c). – ISBN 0-8442-2345-X (p)
    1. Camping–United States–Vocational guidance.   2. Camps–United
States–Employees.   3. Summer employment–United States.   I. Title.
II. Series.
GV198.V63C36   1998
796.54'02373–dc21
                                                                    97-41353
                                                                       CIP

Cover Photo Credits:
Cover photographs by Mark Lamberson, courtesy Swift Nature Camp, Minong, Wisconsin, (630) 654-8036.

Published by VGM Career Horizons
An imprint of NTC/Contemporary Publishing Company
4255 West Touhy Avenue, Lincolnwood (Chicago), Illinois 60646-1975 U.S.A.
Copyright © 1998 by NTC/Contemporary Publishing Company
Printed in the United States of America
International Standard Book Number: 0-8442-2344-1 (cloth)
                                                0-8442-2345-X (paper)
15   14   13   12   11   10   9   8   7   6   5   4   3   2   1

DEDICATION

To lifelong friend and big sister,
Ellen Raphaeli,
who made my first overnight camp experience more than special.

CONTENTS

ABOUT THE AUTHOR

A full-time writer of career books, Blythe Camenson's main concern is helping job seekers make educated choices. She firmly believes that with enough information, readers can find long-term, satisfying careers. To that end she researches traditional as well as unusual occupations, talking to a variety of professionals about what their jobs are really like. In all of her books she includes firsthand accounts from people who can reveal what to expect in each occupation.

Blythe Camenson was educated in Boston, earning her B.A. in English and psychology from the University of Massachusetts and her M.Ed. in counseling from Northeastern University.

In addition to *Opportunities in Summer Camp Careers,* she has written more than two dozen books for NTC/Contemporary Publishing Company.

FOREWORD

Few fields combine such a variety of backgrounds and disciplines as does organized camping. Being a successful camp professional requires skill, vision, and the ability to pursue innovative strategies. Professionals also require some knowledge in very technical fields such as health and nutrition, maintenance, business, and risk management as well as in principles of social group work, recreation, physical education, psychology, and education.

All camp jobs require a considerable personal commitment of time and energy. Camp staff members help foster interpersonal relationships while building a bond between the community and the environment. Camp directors have the unique opportunity to discover the satisfaction that comes from integrating these disciplines while working with people in a stimulating outdoor setting.

I hope this book helps you find your very special place in the camping movement.

Connie Coutellier
Director Professional Development
American Camping Association

ACKNOWLEDGMENTS

The author would like to thank the following camping professionals for providing information about their work:

Rose Balasco, Camp Nurse

Phyllis Bartram, Camp Nurse

Katherine Baum, Arts and Crafts Instructor/Cabin Counselor

Claire Best, Swim Instructor

Diane Boone, Director of Food Service

Lisa Bradley, CIT

Jenn Buczynski, Junior Counselor

Susan M. Burke, Camp Nurse

Julie Casanave, Program Director

Frank Cassisa, Certified Personal Trainer

Beverley Citron, Assistant Cruise Director

Kendall Cutadean, Sports Counselor

Scott Edgecombe, Counselor, Drama Director, Program Director

Angie Hall, General Counselor

Nicole Hebson, Sports Counselor/Assistant Director

Courtney Jackson, Zoo Volunteer

Katie Krieck, Assistant Cook

Tracy Larroude, Camp Director

Rose Elizabeth Ledbetter, Dining Room Staff, Lifeguard

Carol Montague, General Counselor and Swim Instructor

Ellen Raphaeli, General Counselor

Debbie Siu, Junior Counselor

Roberta Updegraff, Church Youth Leader

Jonathan Werner, Camp Cook

CHAPTER 1

THE WORLD OF CAMPS

Many of us have been lucky enough to have spent our summers enjoying the activities and atmosphere that both resident and day camps offer. Out in the fresh air almost twenty-four hours a day; swimming, boating, and playing volleyball; performing skits and working on crafts projects; scoffing up meals in the dining hall with an incredible appetite; enjoying the camaraderie and team spirit; singing camp songs by the fire at night—these are all memories many of us share. And if you're reading this book, you probably want to find a way to participate in these activities again and bring similar memories to a younger generation.

WHY A CAMP JOB?

Camp jobs will give you skills future employers will be impressed to see, skills such as responsibility, maturity, leadership. Some camp jobs can even offer you college credit. Check with your adviser or the guidance office for more details on that.

You could spend your summer in a variety of ways—flipping hamburgers, pumping gas, or hanging around the house getting bored. A camp job lets you get paid doing the activities you love to do. What are the other pluses? You can make friends from around the world and become a hero to a young child. Not such a bad deal.

The American Camping Association defines camp as a "sustained experience which provides a creative, educational opportunity in group living in the outdoors. It utilizes trained leadership and the resources of the natural surroundings to contribute to each camper's mental, physical, social and spiritual growth."

Even if you never spent a day as a camper, you might be considering a career in recreation or have a special skill you'd like to be able to pass on. Summer camps and other related facilities offer an abundance of opportunities to do just that.

THE HISTORY OF SUMMER CAMPS

Summer camps for children have been a part of the American experience for more than 130 years. In the mid-1800s Americans clustered in cities along the eastern seaboard began searching for opportunities to enjoy the great outdoors and open spaces that lay just beyond. In 1861 Headmaster Frederick W. Gunn of the Gunnery School in Connecticut came up with the idea to take students on summer outings. After three successful seasons, he opened a permanent summer camp on a lake that stayed in operation for twelve years.

Gunn inspired others to follow suit, and it was not long before private individuals, church groups, and social service agencies established summer camps. Currently more than six million children benefit from a summer camp experience each year.

SOME FACTS AND FIGURES

Throughout the United States there are approximately 8,500 camps, 5,500 of which are resident (overnight) camps and 3,000 are day camps. Summer day camps have grown by almost 90 percent in the last twenty years. Family camp programs have increased by more than 500 percent in the last twelve years.

According to a survey conducted annually by the American Camping Association, enrollment in camps is up 15 percent from the previous year. Of the six million reported campers, more than a million of those are physically or emotionally challenged, as well as economically disadvantaged.

Each summer approximately 500,000 jobs are filled by high school and college students, teachers, doctors, nurses, sports specialists, waterfront instructors and safety professionals, food service staff and directors, and many others who strive to make a positive impact on the lives of six million children.

Most camps begin their summer season in late May or early June and run until the middle or end of August. Few camps are open after Labor Day.

In the spring and fall, some camps are used for environmental education programs for children. Some offer workshops and seminars in teamwork, communications, and other workplace issues to corporations and business organizations.

THE DIFFERENT KINDS OF CAMPS

Approximately 6,200 of America's 8,500 summer camps, both resident and day camps, are sponsored or run by social service agencies and nonprofit groups such as the YMCA/YWCA, Boy Scouts of America and Girl Scouts of the U.S.A., religious organizations, and Camp Fire Boys & Girls, Inc. Others are operated by school systems or are privately owned.

The camp's sponsorship often determines the philosophy and focus of the camp. For example, some Christian or Jewish camps will provide religious training as a context in which other camp-related activities are conducted; Girl or Boy Scout camps might focus more on outdoor living skills while teaching the philosophy of the particular organization.

In general, camps can be divided into two broad categories: day camps and resident or overnight camps. Within those categories you will find camps with different philosophies and focuses. For example, some camps, both day and resident, believe in providing a general camping experience, covering a wide range of activities; others will focus on one or two specific activities, such as fitness, horseback riding, or computers.

Here are some definitions as outlined by the American Camping Association:

Camp and camping: a sustained experience that provides a creative, recreational, and educational opportunity in group living in the out-of-doors, utilizing trained leadership and the resources of natural surroundings to contribute to each camper's social, physical, and spiritual growth.

Day camping: encompasses the above definition within a framework wherein the camper spends an established period during the day at camp, then returns home each evening.

Resident camping: offers the same benefits in a setting in which the camper lives at one site for a period of at least two or more consecutive nights.

Trip camping: offers programs in which groups move from site to site, whether by their own power or by utilizing a vehicle or animal, e.g., canoes, horses, bicycles, etc.

Family camping: offers organized programs for families in a resident setting. (It does not refer to family campgrounds.)

CAMP PROGRAMS

Within the overall day or resident category, here is a list of the different types of programs/focuses you can expect to find:

academics
archery
arts and crafts
astronomy
athletics
aviation
backpacking
basketball
boating
canoe building
caving
christian emphasis
circus arts
computer
conservation
dance
day trips
dulcimer making
environmental studies
equestrian/horseback riding
fine arts
fitness
golf
gymnastics

hot air ballooning
in-line skating
Jewish emphasis
marine biology
martial arts
mountain biking
performing arts
photography
rock climbing
roller hockey
rope courses
sailing
soccer
special needs
survival skills
swimming
technical tree climbing
tennis
videography
weight watchers
wilderness camping
wind surfing
woodworking
zip lines

Arts and crafts is the program most offered at summer camps, followed by swimming, canoeing, hiking, environmental education, and archery.

In response to a new demand and to attract a wider range of campers, many camps are now offering new activities, many of them challenging and adventure activities, such as high and low ropes courses and rock climbing.

JOB TITLES WITHIN CAMPS

Camp Director

This is the person directly responsible for the overall operation of the camp. Duties can include both administration and programming. Some directors work for a length of time longer than the specific camping period. They can be involved in budgeting, fundraising, staff recruitment, training, and other related duties.

Camp Administrator

This position usually has responsibility for more than one camp. For example, an administrator working for the Girl Scouts of U.S.A. might be in charge of all East Coast summer Girl Scout camps and be involved with primarily administrative functions, relying on the camp directors to run each program.

Program Director

This job title may vary from camp to camp, but the person who holds it is usually responsible for planning, coordinating, and administering various programs and events.

programs and watch over recreational facilities and equipment. They help people, usually children, to pursue their interest in crafts, arts, or sports. They enable people to share common interests in basketball, basket weaving, or bodybuilding for their mutual entertainment, physical fitness, and self-improvement.

Counselors organize teams and leagues so young people and adults can practice fair play and good sportsmanship through competitive sports. They also teach people the correct use of equipment and facilities so maximum benefit can be derived from their use without injury.

Camp counselors lead and instruct child and teenage campers in outdoor-oriented forms of recreation, such as swimming, hiking, and horseback riding, as well as camping. Activities often are intended to enhance campers' appreciation of nature and responsible use of the environment.

In addition, counselors provide campers with specialized instruction in activities such as archery, boating, music, drama, gymnastics, tennis, or computers.

In resident camps, counselors also provide guidance and supervise daily living tasks and general socialization.

WORKING CONDITIONS

Being a counselor or recreation worker does not offer the same amusements afforded campers. You'll be working while those in your care engage in leisure time activities.

While the majority of camp and recreation workers put in about forty hours a week, people entering this field should expect irregular hours, with night and weekend work. You might get one day off a week, or two days off every two or three weeks.

Some of the work, especially at day camps, is only part-time, and, of course, by its very nature, many of the jobs are seasonal, offering work for just two to three months of the year and leaving you without employment in the winter. This schedule, of course, makes camp work attractive to college students, who often have their summers free.

Other related settings, such as YMCA facilities or cruise lines, might offer more full-time employment. (See Chapter 10 for more information on employment in settings other than camps.)

Camp counselors and other recreation workers often spend much of their time outdoors and may work under a variety of weather conditions. Supervisors, administrators, kitchen, and medical workers, on the other hand, may spend most of their time indoors and, therefore, engage in less physical activity. However, for counselors out in the front lines, as is the case for anyone engaged in physical activity, the work can be tiring, and there is always the risk of injury.

ACCOMMODATIONS

Most overnight camps offer free room and board as part of your payment package, but accommodations run the gamut from rustic to luxurious. Some camps provide only tents with no electricity and communal toilet and shower facilities a distance away from your living quarters. Others might have picturesque log cabins with "en suite" bathrooms; still others might offer air-conditioned rooms in a college dormitory or other similar facilities. In most cases, if you are assigned to a group of campers, you'll find yourself bunking in with your charges, with little or no privacy or time to yourself.

Meals are usually served family style in dining halls, and you would be expected to eat with your campers. You might also be assigned dining hall duty, supervising the serving of food and clean up.

TRANSPORTATION

Depending upon the distance from your home to the camp, you might be offered free transportation by bus or plane, or be expected to make your own way to the camp site. Each camp might have different regulations about keeping private cars, so it is a good idea to check on this before you drive yourself.

During the workday, camps usually provide transportation for any camp-related business, but on your days off you might have to fend for yourself.

EMPLOYMENT OUTLOOK

The recreation field has an unusually large number of part-time, seasonal, and volunteer jobs. These jobs include summer camp counselors, lifeguards, craft specialists, and after-school and weekend recreation program leaders. Teachers and college students take many jobs as recreation workers when school is not in session.

Employment of recreation workers is expected to grow faster than the average for all occupations through the year 2005 as growing numbers of people possess both leisure time and the money to purchase leisure services. Growth in these jobs also will be due to increased interest in fitness and health and rising demand for recreational opportunities for older adults in senior centers and retirement communities. Opportunities for part-time and seasonal jobs are expected to be plentiful, but competition is likely for full-time career positions.

Overall job growth in local government where half of all recreation workers are employed is expected to be slow due to budget constraints, and local park and recreation departments are expected to do less hiring for permanent, full-time positions than in the past. As a result this sector's share of recreation worker employment will shrink by the end of the century. Nonetheless, opportunities will vary widely by region, since resources as well as priorities for public services differ from one community to another. Thus, hiring prospects for recreation workers will be much better in some park and recreation departments than overall projections would suggest, but worse in others.

Recreation worker jobs should also increase in the fast-growing social services industry. More recreation workers will be needed to develop and lead activity programs in senior centers, halfway houses, children's homes, and day-care programs for the mentally retarded or developmentally disabled.

Recreation worker jobs in employee services and recreation will continue to increase as more businesses recognize the benefits to their employees of recreation programs and other services such as wellness programs and elder care. Job growth also will occur in the commercial recreation industry, composed of amusement parks, athletic clubs, camps, sports clinics, and swimming pools.

Full-time career job seekers will face keen competition. Because all college graduates, as well as some high school and junior college graduates, can enter recreation worker jobs regardless of their major, applications for career positions in recreation often greatly exceed the number of job openings. Opportunities for staff positions should be best for persons with job experience gained in part-time or seasonal recreation jobs, together with formal recreation training. Those with graduate degrees should have the best opportunities for supervisory or administrative positions.

Prospects are much better for the very large number of temporary seasonal jobs. Demand for seasonal recreation workers is great, and job opportunities should be good. These positions, typically filled by high school or college students, do not generally have formal education requirements and are open to anyone with the desired personal qualities. Employers compete for a share of the vacationing student labor force, and though salaries in recreation are often lower than those in other fields, the nature of the work and the opportunity to work outdoors is nevertheless attractive to many. Seasonal employment prospects should be very good for applicants with specialized training and certification in an activity like swimming. These workers may obtain jobs as program directors.

EARNINGS

Because most work at summer camp is for a short duration, many counselors and other staff members are paid a flat fee for the season. This can be as little as a stipend of a few hundred dollars, including room and board, or can range up to a few thousand, depending upon the facility and its budget. Counselors with specific skills or certificates, such as Water Safety Instructor, generally earn more money than general cabin counselors. Camp nurses or other medical professionals might earn from $800 to $5,000 for the season; kitchen workers, $1,000 to $3,000 for the summer.

Paychecks could be weekly, monthly, or given in full at the end of the season. Although the pay is generally low, the advantage is that during the camping season there are very few expenses and little to spend money on. Most counselors find they save almost their entire paycheck.

Median annual earnings of full-time recreation workers is about $16,000 per year. Earnings of recreation directors and others in supervisory or managerial positions can be much higher—anywhere from $22,000 to $95,000, depending on the level of responsibility and the size of the staff.

Most public and private recreation agencies provide full-time recreation workers with vacation and other benefits such as paid vacation and sick leave and health insurance. Part-time workers receive few, if any, benefits.

CHAPTER 2

QUALIFICATIONS AND TRAINING

Generally the education levels expected for recreation worker jobs range from a high school diploma, or sometimes less for many summer jobs, to graduate education for some administrative positions in large public systems.

When a B.A. or B.S. is required, the usual field of study is within recreation, with an emphasis on camping, group work, liberal arts education, or outdoor or physical education.

Camp counselors with previous camping experience have an edge over those who never attended camp before. Campers who get promoted to CIT (counselor-in-training), then on to junior counselor (both are usually unpaid positions, but might offer a break in or waiver of camp fees) would often have a better shot at a full-fledged counselor position within their camp if an opening occurs than someone from the outside. But because many camps have age requirements for counselors—some will hire eighteen-year-olds, others prefer twenty-year-olds or older—a period of a few years might have to pass before moving from a junior counselor position to a full, paid counselor level.

Full-time career professional positions in recreational settings other than camps usually require a college degree with a major in parks and recreation or leisure studies, but a bachelor's degree in any liberal arts field may be sufficient for some jobs in the private sector.

In industrial recreation, or employee services as it is more commonly called, companies prefer to hire persons with a bachelor's degree in recreation or leisure studies and a strong background in business administration.

Graduates of associate degree programs in parks and recreation, social work, and other human services disciplines also enter some career recreation positions. Occasionally high school graduates are able to enter career positions, but this is not common. Some college students work part-time as recreation workers while earning degrees.

SPECIALIZATIONS

A background with specialized training or experience in a particular field, such as art, music, drama, or athletics, is an asset—and even a requirement—for many jobs.

Some jobs also require a special certificate, such as a Red Cross Senior Lifesaving or WSI (Water Safety Instructor) certificate when there are water-related activities involved. See Chapter 6 for information on Red Cross training.

ADVANCEMENT

Persons with academic preparation in parks and recreation, leisure studies, physical education, fitness management, and related fields generally have better prospects for career advancement, although this varies from one employer to another. In some organizations it is possible to reach the top of the career ladder without a college education, but this is becoming increasingly difficult.

SUPERVISORY POSITIONS

A bachelor's degree and experience are preferred for most recreation supervisor jobs and required for most higher level camp administrator jobs. However, increasing numbers of recreation workers who aspire to administrator positions are obtaining master's degrees in parks and recreation or related disciplines.

Also, many persons in other disciplines, including social work, forestry, and resource management, pursue graduate degrees in recreation.

PROFESSIONAL DEVELOPMENT PROGRAMS

The American Camping Association has developed a curriculum for camp director education. They offer workshops and seminars in the following areas:

Basic Camp Director Course
Camp Director Institute
Program Director Course
Site Manager Course

Here are examples of what some of the programs cover:

New Directors Orientation

A special two-and-a-half-day session for new camp directors, assistant directors, or people who have been in other administrative positions and are considering directing camp in future summers. The program provides an overview of all the aspects of the director's job. It also helps identify the human and material resources needed to direct a camp.

Basic Camp Directors Course

This is a five-day course for camp directors with less than five years experience. The course is designed to present specific content in fourteen management areas:

child and youth development
risk management

health care
special populations
site and facilities
role of the camp director
staffing
philosophy and objectives
organizational design
program
business and finance
marketing and public relations
food service
evaluation

Learning sessions focus on real situations, problems, and solutions.

Camp Director Institute

This is a five-day course for experienced camp directors. Participants must have completed the BCDC (Basic Camp Director Course) and have at least three years experience as a director with overall responsibility for the operation and management of a camp or conference center, or six years experience as a director.

CDI participants examine, refine, and demonstrate consistency between their camp or conference center philosophy and operational components through small group presentation and a critique process.

Program Director Course

This is a five-day course for new and experienced program directors that explores areas such as: philosophy and objectives, camper growth and development, program activities and organization, evaluation, special populations, and health and safety.

Outdoor Living Skills Instructor Course

Outdoor Living Skills Instructor Course (OLS) is for camp specialists, agency staff, or volunteers who have documented experience in outdoor living skills and wish to become an instructor for program leaders that will be teaching the OLS program to campers.

The purpose of the OLS program is to help campers and program leaders gain the skills and attitudes needed for meaningful outdoor experiences with minimum impact on the environment.

For information on these programs contact

Director of Professional Development
   American Camping Association
   5000 State Road 67 North
   Martinsville, IN 46151-7902

Many national youth associations offer training courses for camp directors at the local and regional levels. Contact the individual groups for more information. Their addresses are listed in Chapter 3 and in Appendix A.

Programs leading to an associate or bachelor's degree in parks and recreation, leisure studies, or related fields are offered at about 350 colleges and universities. Many also offer master's or doctoral degrees in this field.

In 1996 approximately ninety bachelor's degree programs in parks and recreation were accredited by the National Recreation and Park Association (NRPA) in cooperation with the American Association for Leisure and Recreation (AALR). Contact the NRPA for a list of these programs. Their address is provided in Appendix A.

Accredited programs offer broad exposure to the history, theory, and philosophy of park and recreation management. Courses offered include community organization, supervision and administration, recreational needs of special populations such as older adults or the disabled, and supervised fieldwork. Students may specialize in areas such as therapeutic recreation, park management, outdoor recreation, industrial or commercial recreation, and camp management.

CERTIFICATION

Certification for this field is offered by the National Recreation and Parks Association (NRPA) National Certification Board and the American Camping Association. The NRPA, along with its state chapters, offers certification as a Certified Leisure Professional (CLP) for those with a college degree in recreation, and as a Certified Leisure Technician (CLT) for those with fewer than four years of college. The American Camping Association offers a certification program for camp directors. Continuing education is necessary to remain certified in either field. Addresses for both the National Recreation and Parks Association and the American Camping Association are provided in Appendix A.

Certification is not usually required for employment or advancement in this field, but it is an asset. Employers choosing among qualified job applicants may opt to hire the person with a demonstrated record of professional achievement represented by certification.

PERSONAL QUALITIES YOU'LL NEED

People planning recreation careers should be outgoing, good at motivating people, and sensitive to the needs of others. Good health and physical fitness are required.

Activity planning calls for creativity and resourcefulness. Willingness to accept responsibility and the ability to exercise good judgment are important qualities because recreation personnel often work without close supervision.

Part-time or summer recreation work experience while in high school or college may help students decide whether their interests really point to a human services career. Such experience also may increase their leadership skills and understanding of people.

Individuals contemplating careers in recreation at the supervisory or administrative level should develop managerial skills. College courses in management, business administration, accounting, and personnel management are likely to be useful.

PREPARING FOR A CAREER IN CAMPING

The American Camping Association offers a professional development calendar that lists programs and courses throughout the country that can help prepare you in addition to any college training you participate in. Courses run the gamut from CPR and first aid; archery instruction; health and safety management; and adapting environmental education materials for students with physical, developmental, and behavioral disabilities; to low ropes and climbing walls courses.

As mentioned earlier, experience as a camper is invaluable to prepare you for a job or career in camping. College students can opt for camp jobs to fulfill internship or field work requirements and some may qualify as work-study positions.

As you work your way up the ladder in a camping career it is a good idea to work in as many different types of camps under different sponsorships as possible, each serving a different clientele.

CHAPTER 3

LANDING THAT JOB

The best advice camping professionals will give you is to start early to find that job. Many jobs are lined up as much as a year in advance; they are taken by counselors and other staff members who plan to work every summer for a particular camp. But starting during the winter months can work for you, too. Waiting until the spring for a summer start date might find you jobless. However, having said that, often last minute openings come up because people's plans do change. So, if you didn't realize you needed a head start, you might still be able to find something by picking up the phone and making a few calls.

WHERE TO LOOK

National Organizations

The following national organizations offer camping programs and provide listings of camp vacancies upon request. When you make contact with them, be specific about the employment information you are seeking and the geographic location in which you would like to work. Some of these organizations accept resumes and will forward them to local councils.

4-H Extension Service
   3860 S Building USDA
   Washington, DC 20250-0900

Boys and Girls Clubs of America
   771 First Avenue
   New York, NY 10017

Boy Scouts of America
   1325 Walnut Hill Lane
   P.O. Box 152079
   Irving, TX 75015-2079

Camp Fire Boys and Girls, Inc.
   4601 Madison Avenue
   Kansas City, MO 64110

Christian Camping International
   P.O. Box 646
   Wheaton, IL 60189

Girl Scouts of USA
   420 Fifth Avenue
   New York, NY 10018-2702

Jewish Welfare Board
   15 East Twenty-sixth Street
   New York, NY 10016

Young Men's Christian Association (YMCA)
   101 North Wacker Drive
   Chicago, IL 60606

State and Local Offices

Call local YMCAs, JCCs, district church offices and councils, other religious organizations, state tourism departments, and local chambers of commerce for names and addresses of camps. These contacts might sponsor their own summer camping programs or know of other sponsors.

Departments of Education

Contacting state departments of education can lead you to school-sponsored camps and related programs.

Colleges and Universities

Within the parks, recreation, leisure, and outdoor education departments of colleges and universities you might find sponsored camping programs with vacancies.

Publications

The American Camping Association compiles the *Guide to Accredited Camps,* which provides information on private, agency, and church-sponsored camps across the United States. The guide gives contact names and addresses and describes the types of programs and the populations they serve. To order this publication contact:

American Camping Association Bookstore
    5000 State Road 67 North
    Martinsville, IN 46151-7902
    or call (800) 428–CAMP.

The American Camping Association also publishes *Camping Magazine,* a bimonthly that runs ads in the classified and professional placement sections for camp positions wanted and camp positions vacant. And every January/February it releases the *Summer Camp Employment Opportunity Book.* To obtain either of these employment information sources contact:

Advertising Manager
    American Camping Association
    5000 State Road 67 North
    Martinsville, IN 46151-7902

On-line Directories

For those of you with a computer and a modem, sources for camping jobs are just a few keystrokes away. The American Camping Association, Peterson's, and other organizations maintain web sites that list current vacancies, including detailed information about the camp and job openings, as well as contact addresses.

At some of the sites you can search databases for jobs broken down by skill areas or location and E-mail your information directly to the camp professional responsible for recruiting.

You can use your own search engine to find the large number of available sites, or try the web site addresses given here to get you started:

http://www.greatsummerjobs.com/search2.html

This site is called Great Summer Jobs and is geared toward helping college students find camp positions. Depending on the time of the year you visit it, you will find current job listings or a suggestion to come back in November when openings are first posted. The site offers a database you can search by camp location, skill, and job description. You also will be able to E-mail your information to the director of the summer program you want to apply to. There is also a link there to Peterson's Education and Career Center, where you'll find information about educational and cultural opportunities for students and adult learners.

http://careers.petersons.com/CJ$BldSrchForm.Summer_Jobs

This site leads you directly to the joint Peterson's and American Camping Association's database, where you can begin your job search by type of position and geographic location.

http://www.petersons.com/summerop/sumsum.html

This site gives you Peterson's Summer Opportunities Database for academic, travel, and camping programs. It lists "various pathways to thousands of terrific camps, academic programs, sports clinics, arts workshops, internships, volunteer opportunities, and travel adventures throughout North America and other continents. Included for hundreds of camps are in-depth descriptions, photographs, personal messages from directors and owners, applications, and on-line brochures."

Also at the site is a link to the American Camping Association's on-line *Directory of Accredited Camps.* It provides information on the ACA and general information about day and resident camps that have complied with the ACA's standards.

http://www.aca-camps.org/search.html

This site takes you to the American Camping Association's complete camp database, where you can search by state for type of camp (resident or day boys' camps, girls' camps, coed camps, and family camps), fees for campers, and any specialty clientele they service. Also there is a link to the summer job database.

Camping Employment Agencies

Employment agencies specializing in camp positions can be found both on- and off-line. On-line, use your favorite search engine; off-line check in your *Yellow Pages* under "employment."

SAMPLE JOB DESCRIPTIONS

The following are meant as examples of the type of job descriptions you will find as you begin your search. Camp names and contact addresses have been omitted because the positions advertised are filled.

Description of Job: Summer in the mountains: private, Jewish coed camp in western North Carolina is seeking experienced cabin counselors. Must be enthusiastic, caring college students and graduates.

Salary: $450–$1,500, based on education and experience
Minimum Age: 18
Start Date: June

Description of Job: Girl Scout camp located in northern Virginia seeks health professionals responsible for all health, medical, and emergency care. Must be qualified RNs, paramedics, or EMT specialists.

Salary: $2,044–$2,644
Minimum Age: 21
Start Date: June 15
Stop Date: August 15
Room/Board: Yes
Transportation: Yes

Description of Job: Easter Seal Camp dedicated to working with people of all ability levels is seeking additional assistant director to supervise day-to-day operations of camp.

Salary: $2,000–$2,400
Minimum age: 21
Start Date: June 20
Stop Date: August 21
Room/Board: Yes
Transportation: No

Description of Job: Christian Orthodox Church camp seeks additional kitchen staff. Will work three (3) meals a day (M–F), only evening meal on Sunday. Culinary background required to prepare nutritional menus.

Salary: $2,000–$3,000
Minimum Age: 20
Start Date: June 23

Stop Date: August 16
Room/Board: Yes
Transportation: No

Description of Job: Private resident girls' camp in Yellow Spring, West Virginia, seeks archery instructor, a female college or graduate student interested in working in a girls' camp. Must be certified by the American Archery Association.
Salary: $1,800–$2,000
Minimum Age: 20
Start Date: June 8
Stop Date: August 16
Room/Board: Yes
Transportation: Yes

Description of Job: Private girls camp in Portland, Maine, seeks mature, fun-loving staff members who have credentials/ability to teach tap, jazz, ballet, modern dance, creative, and hip-hop.
Salary: $1,000–$3,000
Minimum Age: 18
Start Date: June 20
Stop Date: August 17
Room/Board: Yes
Transportation: Yes

GETTING READY TO GO

Once you have landed that camp job of your choice, and if this is going to be your first camping experience, you might have a few more questions than your interviewer addressed.

For a day camp job, you might be wondering what to wear to work and what kind of gear to bring. For a resident camp job the same questions arise—what to pack and how to pack it all.

Day Camp Gear

Just as campers tote a bag with them each day, packed with their swimsuit and towel and a brown-bag lunch, so can you be properly outfitted. Although the morning might start out warm and sunny, it's a good idea to be prepared for a late afternoon shower or drop in temperature. A plastic, fold-up rain poncho will fit easily into your tote bag. Bring along a change of clothing and a second swimsuit for the afternoon swim session. No one feels comfortable sitting in a wet suit all day. Sweatshirts with hoods and pockets also are good to have on hand.

Resident Camp Gear

Many resident camps do not provide bedding. It's a good idea to check on that before you go, and if it is left to you, a duffel bag packed with two sets of sheets, a pillow, and two warm blankets or a comforter will see you through the summer. A group laundry service is generally provided once or twice a week—and that's why you should make sure all your clothes and linens have name tags sewn on or your name written on them with permanent markers, so you can easily claim any misplaced laundry—so pack accordingly.

Don't forget a good supply of towels. Two or three trips a day to the waterfront will take you through a lot of terry cloth. And though you might only wear socks in your sneakers when playing tennis, at camp with uneven ground and underbrush, you might find a supply of socks good ankle protection.

Here is a list of other items you might not want to do without:

Clothes should be comfortable and durable. Shorts, T-shirts, and jeans are the staples of any camper's or counselor's wardrobe. Have several pairs of shoes with you. Morning dew will go through a lot of canvas sneakers. A pair of sturdy shoes for hiking or horseback riding is a must. Some camps have dances, and you might want to bring a dressier outfit for those occasions or for days off.

Head covering to protect you from the sun and ticks.

Tick and bug repellent to discourage mosquitoes, the mainstay of most summer camp locations.

Sunscreen and lip cream are especially essential for waterfront staff.

Flashlight with fresh batteries.

Camera with film and flash for night-time activities.

Canteen or water bottle for hiking or high-activity sports.

Stationery and stamps for those important communications. It's a good idea to purchase the self-adhesive stamps. Humid, damp camp locations can render pre-glued postage stamps useless.

Medication and toiletries and any other personal items you will need. Make sure to get any prescriptions filled before you head out to camp.

The American Camping Association suggests that you do not bring radios, televisions, portable CD players, stereos, food, hunting knives, or expensive clothes.

CHAPTER 4

CITs, JUNIOR COUNSELORS, AND VOLUNTEERS

CITs

CIT stands for counselor-in-training, and the position usually goes to someone who has been a camper at the particular camp. Most camps have an age requirement of about fourteen before they will promote a camper to a CIT rank.

CITS usually participate in all the same activities the campers do, but in addition, they have added responsibilities, helping out senior counselors and supervising the younger campers.

Most CIT jobs are unpaid, but the CIT usually gets to attend the camp for free, with room and board included.

JUNIOR COUNSELORS

Junior counselors are usually a year or two older than CITs. Many camps prefer their junior counselors to be at least fifteen years of age. Duties will vary from camp to camp, but most junior counselors are assigned to one counselor, whom they will assist for the season.

Junior counselors can be in charge of the daily activities of a particular group of campers or work only with a specific activity, such as in the arts and crafts room or at the pool or waterfront.

Salaries for Junior Counselors

Many junior counselor positions are unpaid, waiving the camp fees and providing room and board at resident camps. Some day camps do pay an hourly wage—usually the minimum wage—and overnight camps often offer a $200 or $300 stipend for the summer. A stint as a junior counselor can often be a foot in the door for a fully paid counselor position the following summer.

VOLUNTEERS

Although the formal, academic training you will receive later on is vital to your resume for future career placement, hands-on experience is of equal importance. Not only does it provide a host of significant skills, it also allows the career explorer to make an informed decision about the suitability of camping or recreation work.

Many unpaid volunteers assist paid counselors and other recreation workers. The vast majority of volunteers serve as activity leaders at local day-camp programs, or in youth organizations, camps, nursing homes, hospitals, senior centers, YMCAs, and other settings. Other volunteers function similarly to CITs or junior counselors. Some volunteers serve on local park and recreation boards and commissions.

A person who starts with a term of volunteer work, even before beginning a college program, will have a better idea of what career options camps and recreation facilities have to offer and whether these options are right for him or her. Even if you have spent every summer as a camper, a camper's experience is different from the professional counselor's. Volunteering at a camp is a good way to see things from the other side of the playing field.

One of the biggest benefits of volunteer experience, either through part-time work during the school year or a summer job, is that it often may lead to a full-time job. Volunteers are often the first to hear about openings, and employers often prefer to hire someone they know and already have experience working with.

Getting Started with Volunteer Work

The easiest way to volunteer your time is to call a camp or sponsoring organization and ask to speak to the volunteer coordinator. He or she will work with you to match your interests with the camp's needs.

Volunteer programs are usually flexible about the number of hours and days per week they expect from their volunteers.

FIRSTHAND ACCOUNTS

Lisa Bradley, CIT

Lisa Bradley, a sophomore in high school, is currently in her second year as a CIT at a resident camp in the lakes region of New Hampshire.

HOW LISA GOT STARTED

"I was a camper here first, for three years, and I attended for the full summer session—eight weeks—every year. Last summer, during my third year as a camper, we had our usual morning flag raising. The director always has announcements to make and one morning he announced that I was promoted to a floater. In a way that meant I became a counselor-in-training.

"I guess my parents got the rest of the summer free for me, but I am not sure about that. Basically, as a floater, I had to fill in whenever a CIT had some time off. I'd take over her cabin and supervise her kids for an activity—or sometimes in the evening I had to babysit when she had the evening off.

"It was kind of boring, and I really wanted to have my own cabin of kids. At the beginning of my second summer I was promoted to a full CIT. At this camp you had to be there at least two years and be fifteen before you could be a CIT."

WHAT THE JOB IS LIKE

"At my camp every cabin has six campers, a full counselor, and a CIT. We also have one cabin of floaters. The floaters don't have to have a counselor with them, so that was the best part about that—we had a lot of fun. Now, though, I am in a cabin with six eight-year-olds. They are a bunch of good kids, but a handful, too. Someone is always pulling pranks or giggling at night when she is supposed to be sleeping. Or sometimes two of the girls have a fight and you have to try to help them make up with each other. Once someone was really homesick, and I spent a lot of time trying to make her feel better. She eventually got over it and started to enjoy herself. That made me feel good.

"I help the counselor out and participate in all the activities. I swim laps during instructional swim, and sometimes during free swim in the afternoon, I can sneak off and have an extra nap or just write some letters and have some quiet time.

"But it's usually pretty busy. I have to play games with the kids and help them get dressed and take them to the showers. If someone has to see the nurse, I take her there, too.

"I get to go horseback riding and on canoe trips. The canoe instructor is teaching me how to teach, so maybe next year I can be hired as a junior counselor and help out with the canoe classes instead of going to all the different activities.

"I like the evening campfires the best. We sing songs or tell ghost stories and laugh a lot. I like walking back to the cabin at night when the moon is out and you don't even need to use your flashlight.

"The only thing I don't like about it is that it's an all-girl camp and the boys' camp is way across the lake. We only get together for one dance during the summer, so we never really get to know those boys. One night, though, a couple of the CITs took a canoe out without permission and met some of the boy CITs in the middle of the lake. They got in trouble, though, and got sent home early."

ADVICE FROM LISA

"I have no idea what I am going to do when I finish college, but I do know that going to camp, first as a camper, then as a CIT, really teaches you a lot about being with other people and teamwork. You learn a lot about yourself and a lot of skills, too. I'm a really good swimmer and horseback rider now. I think it's a good experience for anyone to have. And especially, if you live in the city, it's really nice to be out in the woods by a lake every year. Working at a summer camp is a lot better than being a waitress or something like that. I'd advise anyone to give it a try."

Jenn Buczynski, Junior Counselor

Jenn Buczynski works at Lynbrook Summer Playground-Day Camp in New York. She began volunteering when she was fourteen, and in 1997 began her first paying job as a junior counselor.

The camp is based on the grounds of a grammar school. Facilities include a playing field, a gym, an art room, and a computer room.

HOW JENN GOT STARTED

"I needed to do some volunteer work for school and thought it would be a good idea to work at a camp. It's a good summer job, it's only three hours a day, and it's an easy job and keeps me busy.

"There were no real requirements to get the volunteering position I started with; you just needed to be going into the ninth grade or be fourteen years old. I volunteered for two years, then got my current job as a junior counselor. To become a junior counselor at this camp, you need to volunteer first for two years and you also need to be at least sixteen years old."

WHAT THE JOB'S REALLY LIKE

"It's actually really easy. I have about twenty girls, all third graders, to watch every day. It's only three hours a day, fifteen hours a week, and I have a counselor and a volunteer also in my group, so I really don't have to do much. I just have to keep an eye on everyone, help the counselor, or bring the kids to the nurse or to the bathroom.

"It's a great summer job—especially since I'm getting paid for doing close to nothing. I make about $5.20 an hour. Plus, I get ice cream every day, go on trips for free, and get to hang out with my friends.

"A lot of my friends work at my camp, so we usually play a game with the girls and get all the junior counselors to play, too.

"I also have to get the campers their snack. Then we either go to the gym, art room, or to the computer room. Sometimes we play in the playground or watch a movie. I play games with them and just keep an eye on everyone. It can get boring. My kids are mostly really good, and I don't have to watch them that much.

"The counselors are generally really friendly, with a few exceptions. But my counselor is especially funny. The volunteer who works with us is just like one of the kids. She wonders off and plays with the kids, and sometimes we feel as if we are babysitting her, too.

"Some of the kids I'd love to kill, but most of them are good and listen. The ones who don't listen, you practically have to scream at them to get them to even notice that you're talking to them. And then they still don't listen to you. Like today—this little boy in the second grade was bothering my girls, so I told him to stay away from them, but he called me a dirty name!"

ADVICE FROM JENN

"My advice would be to take a CPR and first-aid class. It's always good to stay up to date on that.

"Volunteer for a couple of years to get the feel for having to watch all those kids. Make sure you like the job before you take it and realize too late you can't handle it. You have to feel comfortable."

Debbie Siu, Junior Counselor

Debbie Siu started her first job as a junior counselor the summer of 1997 when she was going into the eleventh grade. She works at Meadowbrook Country Day Camp in Chester, New Jersey.

WHY DEBBIE CHOSE CAMP WORK

"I love kids and I want to get experience working with people. I am not really thinking of a career with children later on, but I do want to earn some money and get to know how to work with people.

"My cousin goes to the same camp, and the office people asked me if I wanted to work there. I went to an interview and got hired."

WHAT THE JOB IS REALLY LIKE

"The camp is very pleasant—the work atmosphere, as well as the grounds. It is surrounded by woods and has a large field where we can play football, lacrosse, baseball, soccer, and other games. It has three swimming pools, six tennis courts, a bullfrog pond, an Indian village, an archery range, an arts and craft building, a ceramics building, a computer room, and other activities such as music, dance, nature, drama, bumper boats, boats, and fishing.

"Junior counselors usually have to take the kids to the rest room, or to the nurse, and run small errands. We have to do lots of walking, and there are many interesting activities such as the zipline and tower of power.

"Zipline is where you have to climb up a tree with protective gear on you, then you are hooked onto a line, then you slide. The whole zipline is about 50 feet long.

"The tower of power is where you have to climb onto a wall. You will have protective gear on you, and instructors will be there to guide you through the whole process. The wall has wooden blocks for you to grab hold of.

"I sometimes have to organize the sports, for example, by separating the children into groups and teaching them how to play something.

"During lunch we are supposed to help them pour drinks. If a kid has to leave early, I will take him to the office and wait for the parents to come.

"Sometimes when the senior counselor asks you to go to the office to hand in something, you just go.

"I also supervise the kids on the playground and during swimming. Every counselor has to go into the pool to help the instructor out."

A TYPICAL DAY

"In a typical day we do activities such as swimming, arts and crafts, soccer, street hockey, and music. I help with the kids, encourage them, and participate in activities with them.

"The bus picks me up at 7:45 A.M. We get to the camp at 8:45. Then I have to sign in and go to my group. I supervise them and sometimes, if the kids want to go to the playground, I have to take them.

"At around 9:15 we do the flag salute and the head counselor makes any announcements.

"Then we go to the changing room to put bags away. The assistant senior counselor and I take the lunches up to the fridge. Then after that, we start our day.

"On Monday the first thing that we do is football. (We start with different activities on different days.) So we will go to the field, and the counselor will teach the kids how to play or organize some kind of game. Then after football, we go to bumper boats. We usually ask the kids to form a line with a partner so we can be more organized.

"After bumper boats, we have instructional swim. We all have to go into the pool.

"After swim, we have lunch. After lunch, we have tennis with the tennis instructor. Sometimes we have to the balls to the kids.

"After tennis, we have electives. Elective time is an hour where kids can pick whatever they want to do. If the kid wants to do swimming as her elective, she has to stick with it for two weeks. Then we change after two weeks.

"After electives, we go to baseball. But sometimes we skip that because it is too hot outside. Then instead we go to the playground.

"After that, the kids have free swim where they can do whatever they want. After free swim, we are supposed to do mini-golf, but sometimes we have snack instead.

"After that we have arts and craft. After arts and craft we tell the kids to get their bags, and we head to the bus stops. Then we all go home. The end of the day is 4:00 P.M.

"It is always busy. And I get frustrated sometimes because kids don't really listen to me. I work five days a week. Each day is from 9:00 A.M. to 4:00 P.M. and sometimes the day can be a little too long.

"But I like it that the kids love to play with you and that they respect you."

SALARY

"The pay at my camp is really cheap—$350 for the whole summer, if you are a first-year junior counselor. Second-year counselors get $550."

ADVICE FROM DEBBIE

"If you want to be a counselor at a camp, you have to love what you are doing. You've got to love kids or else you won't be able to stand it."

CHAPTER 5

GENERAL COUNSELORS

DUTIES

General counselors at both resident and day camps are usually placed in charge of a small group of approximately five to seven campers. The campers are usually of the same age, the range of which depends upon the camp. In general, camps will accept children from the age of three up to age fifteen or sixteen. If you have a preference for a particular age range with which you would be comfortable working, then this should be taken into consideration when applying for jobs at particular camps.

A general counselor will usually spend most of the day with his or her charges, escorting them to various activities, such as scheduled swimming or sporting lessons. At some camps, while the campers are participating in a particular activity that a specialty counselor supervises, the general counselor might be offered a free period during that time. At other camps, or for particular activities, the general counselor will be expected to participate and help supervise.

General counselors usually spend mealtimes with their charges, dining at the same table, supervising behavior as well as contributing to the overall fun atmosphere camps strive to foster.

General counselors, especially those with young children as charges, will also supervise taking trips to the showers and toilet facilities, dressing, making beds, gathering clothes for the laundry, and various other day-to-day tasks of living.

Night-duty schedules at resident camps will vary from camp to camp, but general counselors should expect to be on hand several evenings a week, if not most evenings, to supervise their own charges, as well as the charges of other counselors during nights off.

SCHEDULING

Days and other periods off, as mentioned in Chapter 1, will vary from camp to camp. But in general counselors should not expect a lot of free time during their seasonal job.

Day camps usually operate on a Monday through Friday basis, giving the counselor his or her weekends and evenings free. Duties would generally be the same during the day for day camp counselors as for resident counselors, with the possible added responsibility of supervising transportation to and from the camp. This means that counselors will have to account for all their charges getting on and off the camp buses.

SALARIES FOR GENERAL COUNSELORS

As mentioned in Chapter 1, salaries are far from glamorous for camp counselors. Day camp counselors can be paid an hourly rate, sometimes just the minimum wage or slightly above that, or given a flat fee for the summer.

Counselors at overnight camps will be provided with free room and board in addition to their summer salary, which can run anywhere from $1,000 to $2,500 for the season.

FIRSTHAND ACCOUNTS

The best way to get a good idea of what it would be like as a general counselor is to hear it from those who have had the experience. The following firsthand accounts will give you a good look at life as a general counselor.

Ellen Raphaeli, General Counselor

Ellen Raphaeli spent one summer—three, three-week sessions and a one-week orientation period—as a general counselor at Camp Kingswood in Bridgton, Maine.

WHAT DREW ELLEN TO CAMP WORK

"I was twenty years old, in the process of transferring out of state for my junior year of college. Since my senior year of high school, I had been working while going to school, and I decided that I wanted to spend this particular summer doing something fun. I had never been to overnight camp as a kid, only to day camp for a few weeks when I was seven, but I had found it all terrifying—the kids, the counselors, and the lake, which smelled like rusty metal. I finally convinced my parents that it wasn't worth having me throw up every morning just to give me an experience I was determined not to have.

"But at twenty, I was ready for camp. I liked kids. And I figured that a summer like this would help me unwind."

HOW ELLEN GOT HER JOB

"My initial intention had been to work at a day camp. There was a day camp sponsored by the local Jewish Community Center, and I thought that would be convenient. I applied for the overnight camp job at Kingswood only because I did not get the day camp job. I filled out a form, I was interviewed, and I got the job."

THE SKILLS ELLEN BROUGHT TO THE JOB

"On my application I said something about my swimming (I was a pretty good swimmer) and that I played the guitar. During the course of the summer, though, I was able to call on a lot of little skills. I knew enough about sketching to take my kids on sketch trips; I knew enough about fencing to pull out some fencing masks that I found in the sports shed and let the kids parry a bit. Another counselor and I organized the unit musical shows— she did the drama and I did the music.

"All counselors worked in some capacity at the waterfront, too, and I taught the intermediate swimmers.

"But, in retrospect, I think my main qualifications were the fact that I really liked kids, and the fact that having never been to camp, I was not jaded. There were three counselors who quit at the end of the first session out of disgust at what they saw as the lack of the kind of facilities they expected from a camp. But for me it was all new. I learned to canoe; I sort of learned something about archery. I got to tell ghost stories at night and make twelve-year-olds scream; and I got to sit in the semidark with a few of my peers and talk about hopes and dreams and fears."

ELLEN'S DUTIES

"Essentially, I was responsible for the five girls in my bunk. I got them up in the morning, tucked them in at night, and guided them through their activities for the day.

"The exceptions were when they were in their swim groups at the waterfront. That's when I had a period off.

"We had a period off each day. Usually three bunks participated in activities together. During some activities two counselors would supervise the three bunks, giving the third counselor an hour or so to read or sleep or write letters or swim.

"A typical day was getting up at reveille, marching to the waterfront to raise the flag, and then going into breakfast. Then there were the activities of the day—some with specialty counselors (arts and crafts, waterfront), but many based on whatever a bunk counselor or a group of three counselors could cook up."

"I still think of that summer as one of the best summers of my life. I enjoyed the camp activities, I enjoyed my fellow counselors, and I enjoyed the campers. There are campers I am still enjoying, who, thirty-five years after that summer, are like family.

"And there are moments I still remember. A kid from another bunk crying in the washroom her first night there. She'd been crying in her bunk, apparently, but her counselor had told her to go wash her face and get herself together. 'What's wrong,' I asked. She'd never been away from home before, she said. Neither had I, I told her. We talked about the difficulties of being away from home for the first time and decided we'd both get through it somehow. She stopped crying, washed her face, gave me a kiss, and ran back to her bunk. I guess that, in general, I tried to do for the campers directly or indirectly in my care what I would have liked someone to have done for me when I was seven and terrified of day camp."

Carol Montague, General Counselor

Carol Montague spent four summers working at various overnight camps in Texas, including a Girl Scout camp and a YWCA camp. (Learn more about her work as a swim instructor in Chapter 6.)

HOW CAROL GOT STARTED

"I started going to camp as a camper in 1971. When I was sixteen in 1978, I entered the CIT (counselor-in-training) program at the camp. Training was two years, four weeks each summer.

"You don't have to have the CIT training I had to be a counselor, though. If you're old enough, you just apply to the organization that owns the camp where you want to work. As for the swimming, you do have to be trained. Most camps prefer the Red Cross training rather than the YMCA training. I've had both, but neither is current any longer."

WHAT THE WORK WAS LIKE

"As a counselor, I did double duty. I had a cabin of kids and I taught swimming.

"Every camp is different. Most deal with nature. The camps along the Brazos River stand mostly on sandstone, covered with oak and white mountain cedar trees. And, of course, it's hot in Texas in the summer. But the facilities differ quite a bit. A typical day, remember, lasts all day, not just eight hours. The morning (after breakfast) is spent taking classes. The afternoon, immediately after lunch, is a two-hour rest period. Then free swim and an afternoon activity. After dinner, another activity. At the larger camps, activities alternate between involving just single cabins, sections (divided by age), or all-camp activities. Once a week there is also a cook out.

"Activities include swimming, horseback riding, arts and crafts, hiking, canoeing, sports and games, archery, nature studies, and more.

"There is something going on all the time, so it never gets boring unless the activity itself is one you don't enjoy. However, it can get tiring. Counselors are generally allowed two hours a day away from their kids while another counselor looks after them. At one of the camps where I worked, we were not allowed off the grounds during those hours. At another, we were."

THE DOWNSIDES

"For me, there was more pressure to the job than I expected. For one thing, as the kids change every week or two, you face a new set of problems. One camper, I recall, opened up to me, telling me the terrible situation she had at home.

"Some kids can become attached to a counselor and cause them trouble after camp, finding their telephone number and, sometimes, calling them to excess. It's happened. But many camps have the counselors choose nicknames so the real name is not known to the camper. I, myself, kept in contact with three of my counselors, none to excess, and I remain friends with all three.

"Sometimes you may find you have a problem with another counselor. I did. My kids were accused of doing something I knew they didn't do. The counselor who accused them would not relent. A week later, she went AWOL.

"The worst part was burnout. To help with that, one camp allowed me one week during which I only taught swim lessons. Also, kids with problems are draining on counselors."

THE UPSIDES

"The thing I liked most was teaching the kids. I also enjoyed joining the kids in activities."

ADVICE FROM CAROL

"Be a camper before you're a counselor. Those who are campers, I think, have a great advantage over those who are not. Campers see how counselors work. They get an idea of what is involved.

"Barring that, it might be helpful to find some volunteer work dealing with children. Whatever you do, don't lose your temper with any child. You'll lose your job in a hurry that way. You must like working with kids.

"Also, most applicants for counselor jobs will need to be at least somewhat competent to teach one or more of the activities offered at camp."

Angie Hall, General Counselor

Angie Hall has had nine years experience as a camper. She works at Camp Tygart, an overnight camp in West Virginia. In 1996 she became a CIT there and a full counselor in 1997, the year she graduated from high school.

HOW ANGIE GOT HER JOB

"I have just graduated from high school and I am going on to college. I have been attending this camp for nine years now, and I always wanted to be a counselor. I worked my way up from being a special camper who does all of the dishes and general cleaning of the camp, to a counselor-in-training between my junior and senior years of high school, to being a full counselor this summer. I got this job because I was associated with the camp for so many years."

WHAT THE CAMP IS LIKE

"It is an overnight camp, where children stay for a week at a time. It runs for four weeks with a one-week orientation period. The children go hiking, camping, horseback riding, and swimming; play tennis and softball; go canoeing and fishing; and practice archery.

"The ages of the children who attend this camp run from seven to fifteen. I get to participate with the campers in a lot of activities. When I work at the horses, we saddle them up and teach the children a little about the parts of a saddle; we show them how to actually saddle and ride a horse.

"With the younger children we walk them around the field on a horse, but with the older children we take them on a thirty- to forty-five-minute trail ride. Usually one counselor is at the front of the line and another is at the end.

"When we play tennis, we feed the children some forehands and backhands and help the children where help is needed. Basically, we teach them skills while they are having fun.

"There is also hiking and camping on Cheat Mountain for the older children. They can go on either a two-day or a three-day trail. Sometimes there is an overnight horse trail or an overnight canoe trail. The younger children also go on overnight trips, but they do not hike as far as the older children.

"Along with hiking and camping the children also do arts and crafts, tennis, field sports, cooperative sports, and nature study."

A TYPICAL DAY

"The day begins with dorm inspection at 8:40 A.M. Breakfast begins at 9:00 and is followed by flag ceremony. Then the first activity period begins. In the morning there are two activity periods, each an hour long.

"After the two periods there is general swim for forty-five minutes. It is followed by lunch and then a rest period.

"After rest period we have canteen, where the children can get a soda and a snack. Then there are two more activity periods, followed by another general swim, and then dinner.

"After dinner the children get to choose their activity, usually swimming, field sports, tennis, or fishing. Then there's another canteen and the evening flag ceremony.

"Afterwards there is a short vespers, and then it is bedtime for the younger children and gym time for the older children.

"It is real busy. The workday goes from 8:30 in the morning until 10:15 at night, when the older children go to bed. But it is the best experience a person can have.

"The downside is that you are so busy that there is very little time for yourself, but that is also a good thing.

"You also make the best friends you'd ever want to have."

DAYS OFF

"As far as time off goes, we spend one week in the dorms where the children sleep and that week we get very little time off. Other than that, we are allowed to do whatever we please after 10:30 P.M., as long as we stay on the property.

"On Saturdays we have to clean out the dorms, and at noon we are done. We do not have to be back on the property until midnight."

SALARY

"We start out at $135 a week, with $100 during orientation week. There is also a $10 raise each season you work."

ADVICE FROM ANGIE

"You need to have a lot of patience and a love for children, as well as tons of energy. You also need to be able to work cooperatively with others."

CHAPTER 6

SPECIALTY COUNSELORS

One of the biggest pluses of camp from the camper's and parent's point of view is that camps help young people discover and explore their talents, interests, and values. Most schools can't satisfy all these needs. According to experts, kids who have had camping experiences end up being healthier and have fewer problems. At camp, children learn to solve problems, make social adjustments to new and different people, and manage responsibility. They also gain new skills that help increase their self-esteem.

THE ROLE OF THE SPECIALTY COUNSELOR

Although general counselors are usually placed in charge of the same small group of campers, supervising them throughout the day and night, often specialty counselors are not responsible for any particular cabin or group of campers, but see all the campers throughout the week.

General counselors will escort their campers to the various activities and programs that the camp has planned for them, and it is at this point that the specialty counselor will take over. Depending on the camp, the general counselor may or may not stay to assist the specialty counselor during that activity period.

Specialty counselors are hired for the special skills they possess and are able to pass on to campers. They may be tennis experts, art majors skilled in arts and crafts, singers, dancers, or equestrians. For every camp program (see Chapter 1 for a list of camp focuses and specialties) a specialty counselor must be on hand to teach and guide the campers.

TRAINING FOR SPECIALTY COUNSELORS

Often no formal qualifications are expected of specialty counselors, other than proven expertise in the area and the ability to instruct others. A physical education major, skilled in a variety of sports, could apply for a sports-related specialty position. In the same vein, a dance student or professional dancer could land a job teaching different forms of dance at a specialty camp.

That rule of thumb, though, does not usually apply to waterfront staff.

WATERFRONT STAFF

Whether situated lakeside or by a pool or even at the ocean, most day and resident camps prominently feature waterfront activities, including swim instruction, water safety, and sometimes boating, as a cornerstone of their summer programs.

Although many specialty camp jobs do not require specific certification, waterfront jobs usually do. Although waterfront activities often can offer the most pleasure—what could be nicer than jumping into a refreshing spring-fed lake to cool off during a hot summer day?—they can also present the most danger. Waterfront staff must be skilled, observant supervisors who are well versed in safety procedures, lifesaving and rescue techniques, and first aid.

Training for Waterfront Staff

Camps seeking to hire swimming and boating instructors and lifeguards, more often than not expect their staff to show proof of professional training and will generally want them to possess Red Cross certification.

Here are some sample Red Cross courses that lead to that certification:

AMERICAN RED CROSS LIFEGUARD CERTIFICATION COURSE

Purpose: To teach lifeguards the skills and knowledge needed to prevent and respond to aquatic emergencies.

Includes: Adult, child, and infant CPR; CPR for professional rescuer; and first aid certification. Must be fifteen years of age and attend every session.

Objectives: Understand the value of behaving in a professional manner. Recognize the characteristic behaviors of distressed swimmers, as well as active and passive drowning victims. Recognize an aquatic emergency and act promptly and appropriately. Apply the equipment-based rescue skills and techniques used by professional lifeguards. Recognize and care for a possible spinal injury. Provide first aid and CPR.

Prerequisites: Must be able to swim 500 yards: 100 yards each of the front crawl, breast stroke, and sidestroke; the stroke(s) used for the remaining 200 yards are the participants' choice. Tread water for two minutes using legs only, crossing arms across the chest. Submerge to a minimum depth of 7 feet, retrieve a ten-pound object, and return to the surface.

Certification requirements: Successfully complete two written exams with a minimum score of 80 percent; complete two final skill scenarios; perform all critical skills.

Course length: Suggested minimum: thirty-three hours (plus a one-and-one-half-hour precourse session).

Certificate validity: Lifeguard training (including first aid): three years. CPR for the professional rescuer: 1 year.

RED CROSS SAFETY TRAINING FOR SWIM COACHES

Purpose: To provide training in aquatic safety for competitive swim coaches and officials, athletic trainers, athletes participating in aquatic activities, aquatic exercise trainers, and others involved in aquatic competition or exercise programs.

Objectives: Understand the safety responsibilities of an aquatic leader. Recognize hazards associated with swimming pools and explain how to eliminate or minimize these hazards. Recognize a swimmer in distress or drowning. Explain and demonstrate rescue skills. Recognize specific medical conditions that pertain to swimmers. Explain and demonstrate in-line stabilization skills for spinal injury management.

Prerequisites: None.

Certification requirements: Successfully complete final skills test and pass written test with a minimum score of 80 percent.

Course length: Suggested minimum: eight hours.

Certificate validity: Three years.

RED CROSS WATER SAFETY INSTRUCTOR CERTIFICATE (WSI)

Purpose: To train instructor candidates to teach the Infant and Preschool Aquatics Program, the seven levels of the Learn to Swim Program, the Community Water Safety and Water Safety Instructor Aide courses, and, for eligible individuals, the Safety Training for Swim Coaches course.

Objectives: Use program materials effectively and plan and conduct effective courses. Evaluate the progress of students for certification. Prepare and submit accurate records and reports.

Prerequisites: Must possess an Instructor Candidate Training certificate issued in the last twelve months or a current Health and

Safety Services instructor authorization and must successfully complete the precourse session consisting of tests of water safety and swimming skills and knowledge.

Certification requirements: Successfully participate in course activities, meet instructor candidate competencies, and pass a written test with a minimum score of 80 percent.

Minimum age: Seventeen by end of course.

Course length: Suggested minimum: thirty-six hours (not including the precourse session).

Certification validity: Authorization is for two calendar years. All authorizations expire on December 31.

For more information on swim instructor, lifesaving, and lifeguard courses, contact your local Red Cross or YMCA.

What a Waterfront Job Is Like

While general counselors will escort their campers to a variety of activities during the day, swimming and boating instructors and lifeguards generally spend the whole day at the waterfront.

Mornings are usually spent in providing scheduled instruction to swimmers of different levels. Depending on how many swim instructors a camp has on staff, you could be responsible for beginner, intermediate, and advanced swimmers, or work with only one particular level.

Class time usually runs for thirty to forty-five minutes, with no breaks in between each group. Swim instructors spend a lot of time in and out of the water—more time in when teaching beginners—and are in direct sunlight for most of the day. Sunscreen and large hats and T-shirts worn over bathing suits are essential gear for any waterfront staff.

Lunchtime and an hour's rest period thereafter are usually scheduled into most camp's activities. In the afternoon, swim instruction can continue, or the camp can offer a play period or a "free swim." During this time either lifeguards or swim instructors doubling as lifeguards take over to supervise the free-swim periods. Depending upon the size of the camp and the number of campers, general counselors also might be scheduled to assist with lifeguarding duties.

As boating instruction can be scheduled throughout the day, boating instructors face the same sun exposure hazards that their swimming instructor counterparts do. In addition boating instructors often have to maneuver canoes or row boats into the water and carry paddles, oars, and life jackets. This all requires physical strength.

At the beginning of the season, the sun, water, and all that fresh air can be tiring for new instructors. All waterfront staff members need to be in good physical health.

Other Duties for Waterfront Staff

Waterfront staff might also be expected to maintain equipment; clean and neaten the waterfront area, including boathouses and storage sheds; ensure proper chlorine levels in swimming pools; and operate boats.

During mealtimes waterfront staff might supervise tables, and in the evening they may be expected to participate in special activities. Waterfront staff also might have night duty for a cabin or group of cabins.

SALARIES FOR SPECIALTY STAFF

Salaries for a general or cabin counselor or similar job generally are from $750 to $2,000 for the camp season. Employees with special skills, such as lifeguard training, may earn up to $3,000, but they often have fewer breaks or rest periods.

Additional benefits also include free housing and meals, free laundry, and sometimes health and accident insurance and free transportation to and from the camp.

And, of course, all counselors gain valuable experience that can be important additions to resumes and that can offer memories to last a lifetime.

FIRSTHAND ACCOUNTS

The following firsthand accounts will give you an idea of what specialty counselor jobs in swimming, sports, and arts and crafts are really like, the upsides as well as the down.

Claire Best, Swim Instructor

Claire Best worked as a swim instructor both at a resident Girl Scout camp and for a metropolitan YMCA.

HOW CLAIRE GOT STARTED

"Between the time I was eight years old and nineteen, I spent almost every summer of my life at a variety of camps, in one capacity or another. I started with day camps, and then at age twelve I was finally allowed to go away to overnight camp. At age fifteen I was made a CIT, counselor-in-training, and at age seventeen I got my first paying camp job, as a swim and canoeing instructor at a Girl Scout camp in Maine. Two years later I was a general counselor at another camp. Even in college I ended up doing similar work in my work-study program, employed by the local YMCA as a swim instructor and also as a youth counselor.

"My years as a camper prepared me for work as a counselor. I had learned a lot of skills, some of which I was later able to help other campers learn. Swimming was my strongest area, and by the time I was sixteen I had passed my Red Cross junior and then senior lifesaver tests. I never did go on for my WSI (Water Safety Instructor), but I was lucky. I was able to find work without it. It helped that at the time the YMCA followed a different swimming program than the Red Cross. These days, though, the more certification you have, the better it is for you."

WHAT THE WORK WAS LIKE

"As a camp swim instructor I spent all day at the waterfront, on the dock or in the water, teaching beginner, intermediate, and advanced swimmers. With the little children, you had to be in the water with them, for their safety and to reassure them and to demonstrate. The older children, who were better swimmers, needed less demonstration, so, if you didn't feel like getting wet on a certain day, you could just set them to swimming laps. I'd call out instructions to help them improve their strokes. By the end of the day, my voice would be hoarse, or I'd feel pretty waterlogged sometimes. But it was a great way to spend the summers—in the sun all day."

THE UPSIDES

"Camp life is what I enjoyed the most. The commotion in the dining hall, living in a rustic cabin in a wooded setting, the campfires at night, the songs, the skits, the sports competitions. And the friendships. They were free and easy days. The salaries were pretty horrendous, but you got room and board and a couple of days off here or there to explore the surrounding area. It was like a paid vacation."

Carol Montague, Swim Instructor

Carol Montague worked both as a general counselor (see Chapter 5) and a swim instructor at various camps in Texas. Here is her account:

"Teaching was usually a joy. My favorite class was the beginner group. Sometimes I had kids who were not afraid of the water but didn't know a proper stroke. Other times I had students who were terrified of the water. I witnessed one such student doing the crawl stroke during free swim. It was terrible—but at the beginning of the week, she wouldn't even put her face in the water.

"Another student, too afraid to swim, a couple of years later, passed with flying colors. Some of these kids do know the crawl to some extent, and I assumed she was one because her stroke was so good. But, no. She said she didn't know it at all before I taught her. It feels so good when you are able to teach children something you love yourself!"

Rose Elizabeth Ledbetter, Lifeguard

Rose Elizabeth Ledbetter worked for two years as a camp lifeguard. (You can also read about her experience working as a part of the camp kitchen staff in Chapter 9.)

"I worked all through my high school and several college summers at camp. I began as a kitchen worker, then moved on to counselor, then I ran a concession, and then the last two years I worked as a lifeguard. The camp began as a Baptist camp, then was opened for all children, and the last two years I was there, it was home to Camp Smile-a-Mile, a camp for children who either had cancer or had survived it.

"As a lifeguard things were a little more relaxed than with other positions I had held. The chlorine had to be tested first thing in the morning, but that only took one person, so we took turns. One of us got up at six-thirty, threw on a suit, tested the levels, and added chlorine. The rest of us slept in.

"We weren't required to show up at breakfast, so we usually slept in until ten or fifteen minutes before the first group of campers hit the pool at nine. Then we'd get up, skip the shower, and put on a suit. The style we adopted was a baseball cap with our hair sticking out the back, a tank-style suit with a sports bra underneath it, and a pair of oversized men's boxer shorts over the suit with the waist rolled down. The one 'must' was a hat. Even those of us with the darkest complexions needed a hat. I'd always thought my fair skin didn't tan, but even with layers of sunscreen, after a few monster burns, I got the tan of a lifetime.

"In the mornings we usually snuck in the kitchen and sweet-talked the staff there into a few leftover breakfast tidbits and then headed down to the pool. After a quick dip to wake ourselves up, we got ready for the campers.

"At the beginning of the season, when the campers first arrived at camp, we made them form a single file line at the gate and then directed them to walk in quietly and sit at the edge of the pool. We gave them the rules of the pool: no horseplay, no running, no diving in the shallow end of the pool, no hanging on the rope, no pushing, no hanging on the lifeguard chair.

"We used the buddy system, pairing up the children (an abhorrent system that doesn't work and always leaves one poor kid without a buddy). One of us climbed up into the chair and the other lined up those who wanted to take the swim test. The test was to swim the length of the pool on the deep side of the rope. That was pretty funny. You wouldn't believe the kids who lied about their swimming abilities to stay with their friends. We also made the counselors take the test after one too many 'grown-ups' lied about their abilities as well.

"Then we sat there looking cool in our shades, swinging our whistles off the ends of our fingers, and watching the campers swim.

"On *Baywatch,* they save three or four people on every show, but the truth is not nearly so exciting. We made only a save or two a week, and most of those were really more panic than drowning. My first real save was a chaperone who'd had a heart attack in the pool. In all of the lifeguarding classes and the CPR classes I'd taken, no one had informed me that a drowning victim could throw up in your mouth when you give them mouth to mouth. It was so gross. I wasn't scared when it was going on, but after everything was okay, and the ambulance had left, I walked out of the fence to a clump of bushes and got sick myself.

"In between scheduled swims, we cleaned the pool. Remember this isn't a home pool. The pool was nearly Olympic-size and the deep end was ten feet. So to clean the pool, we'd throw in a folding metal chair, balance ourselves standing on the back of the chair with our noses barely poking out of the water, and use a brush to reach the bottom. The sides could be cleaned from out of the water, but cleaning the bottom was a miserable job. A person can get hypothermia even in 80-degree water in less than an hour. So we were careful to work in short shifts. Still, the work was exhausting and freezing.

"The last group of campers ended their swim time before dinner, and after dinner the pool was open to staffers and chaperones only. Those were the real fun times. We broke every rule we made the kids follow."

SOME ADVICE FROM ROSE ELIZABETH

"Get in shape before camp begins and make sure you get your certification before summer starts.

"To get your lifeguarding license, you have to be sixteen or eighteen, depending on your state. Only two organizations can give you that license: the Red Cross or the YMCA. Classes cost less than one hundred dollars, but they are tough and time consuming.

"You will be required to know the breast stroke, back stroke, and the side stroke (life-saving stroke) and swim these strokes in timed laps.

"You must be able to swim a certain distance, usually the length of the pool, under water. You must learn several holds and carries, as well as different ways to enter and exit the water.

"You must be able to do the dead man's float for a half hour (lifting your face to breathe as needed) and tread water fully clothed for ten to twenty minutes.

"Even if you are not a lifeguard, many camps require that all staffers know CPR and take a basic first aid course. Some camps offer these classes as a seminar for staffers at the beginning of the summer.

"Working at a camp also looks great on a resume. The job instills more responsibility than running a drive-through or cooking fries. Some camps take counselors on a volunteer basis. When Smile-a-Mile, a program for young cancer victims, came to our camp, I was a lifeguard. Most of the counselors worked for little or no pay. The experience was well worth it. Contact the local children's hospital if you are interested in this sort of work. Many have summer programs like the one I saw."

Nicole Hebson, Sports Counselor/Assistant Director

Nicole started camp work in 1995 and has spent three years at Skokie Park District Outdoor Sports Camp in Illinois. In the summer of 1997, she spent the first session as a counselor and the second session as an assistant director.

She graduated in 1997 from the University of Iowa with a B.A. in English. In the fall of 1997, she started at Northeastern Illinois University, where she is pursuing her secondary education teacher certification and a master's degree program at the same time.

HOW NICOLE GOT STARTED

"I have always enjoyed working with kids. I applied for a job as a counselor and gave them my qualifications—my CPR and first aid certification were really the key. I told them why I thought I would be a good addition to the camp and what I'd have to offer, and I was hired.

"Another thing that was pretty big was that I had been involved in intercollegiate athletics. They were looking for people who specifically had that experience and the ability to teach different sports.

"I knew a few people who were the heads of administration up at the park district. They gave me recommendations, which helped immensely. They knew me from our parish and parochial grade school and all of my involvement in those two areas, and so I'm sure somewhere along the way, that was mentioned.

"I'd have to say that being active in your community, parish, school, or whatever, is one of the best ways to help out a resume."

WHAT THE JOB'S REALLY LIKE

"Honestly, this may be the last year for me. I don't know for sure, but it seems as if it's different than it used to be. The kids, the parents (especially), and the enthusiasm at the park have all changed.

"I guess by different I mean the kids used to be way more athletic. They used to be great, but now it's dramatically different. Here's an example: one of my jobs as an assistant sports director is to get a morning relay going that the whole camp participates in, only we haven't had an all-camp relay in a while because the camp has more than two-hundred campers and only twenty staff—we are way understaffed. The plan was that the kids were to do three cartwheels and sprint to where their counselors were and then on the way back do three somersaults. But the kids could not do the cartwheels—they had no idea how to go about it.

"The gymnastics we were asking them to do weren't that hard, but they had trouble with the somersaults, too. If they had had my school gym teacher, they'd know how to do this stuff. I don't know what gym teachers are teaching them these days.

"Also, a handful of kids do not know how to play many of the sports we play at camp, and in the first two weeks of each session (four weeks a session, two sessions total), we have our counselors run drills and practice skills with the kids to get them acclimated with what we will have them playing in the weeks to come. We try as hard as we can to get the kids ready to compete with one another as well as with other groups in the camp, and they love the competition, but it gets frustrating when they don't want to learn the skills it takes to compete.

"I guess I am coming from the standpoint of being a bit of a jock, but that was why I was hired, and that is why we hire a lot of our counselors. We know their athletic backgrounds and we know they can be effective with kids.

"When I think about the job, I think a lot these days about the people I work with, because many times that's why I go to work. Nine out of ten of our counselors will tell you the same thing. We are a relatively tight-knit bunch. There are about five of us who attended the same university.

"But, the job is a cinch, no matter how much we moan about whatever, it is a cinch. How many jobs allow you to go out and play in the sun all day with a bunch of kids?

"On Mondays you get to go ice-skating for half of the day, on Tuesdays and Thursdays we take the kids to the pool for the morning up until lunch, on Wednesdays we go on field trips to water parks, bowling alleys, batting cages, mini-golf courses, and the best trip—a Cubs game."

Kendall Cutadean, Sports Counselor

Kendall Cutadean works at an athletic club in Broomfield, Colorado, that hosts a sports-day camp every summer for kids ages six to thirteen. He started as a camper, then worked as a junior counselor for two years, and has now been a paid counselor for two years. He is currently a junior in high school.

Camp facilities include a swimming pool, squash and racquetball courts, a gym, a track, an outdoor sand volleyball court, and an indoor "walleyball court" (a racquetball court with a volleyball net built in).

HOW KENDALL GOT STARTED

"I started as an attendee at this camp. I was one of the five people who attended it the very first year it opened. I kept going to camp every summer, until I was trained to be a junior counselor. I was not paid for this work, but I had some authority and was allowed to attend for free. After two years being a junior counselor, I became a full-time counselor, in 1996.

"What attracted me to work in a day camp was that I liked the idea of teaching and promoting various sports, seeing as how that is my life. I play soccer for a competitive club team called F. C. Boulder. We are in the top division in the state, known as Premier. I plan to play in the future. My goal is to make it to college soccer, major league soccer, and my lifelong dream is to play for the U.S. National Team. I will continue to practice and work hard in order to fulfill my goal.

"I got my first sport camp job by calling the athletic director at the club (he knew me very well). I told him I was interested and ready to have a job there."

WHAT KENDALL'S JOB IS LIKE

"This camp involves many different kinds of sports, games, and activities that keep the children involved and in shape throughout the summer. We are very fortunate to use the fine facilities at the club.

"My job is fun on some days, and very difficult on others. It is mainly in the hands of the kids. If they want to be disruptive and disrespectful, they will. But that is usually not the case. Most days are filled with various sports, which I enjoy teaching and participating in.

"I have a wide variety of duties. As a counselor I am responsible for the safety of the kids and to make sure everyone is having a good time. We don't like to have kids not participate; we try our best to get all people involved.

"Also, we try to ensure that parents feel safe about leaving their kids with us. It is required for every counselor to be certified in first aid and CPR."

A TYPICAL DAY

6:30 A.M. Open to all "early bird" campers
"One counselor will be there at 6:25, waiting for those early campers. The first kid gets to pick out a movie, and we will watch it to its end. After the movie, usually enough kids have arrived to start playing games."

8:00 Go to gym and let campers decide on a game
"The game of choice is usually a dodgeball game, which everyone is eager to play. If the game is running well, we will continue with it until 9:00, which is when we start the formal schedule."

9:00 Take attendance and lunch order forms, and divide campers into three groups
"The attendance is for the athletic director, to ensure that everyone is paid for. The club is nice enough to offer lunch menus, from which the kids can order lunch for great prices. We divide the kids into three groups and they participate in three different 'rotations.'"

9:30 Rotations
"Each of the three rotations is forty minutes. One or more counselors teach each rotation.

One rotation is in the gym. Usually there is a theme for the week. Early in the week we teach fundamentals and end the week with full-fledged games.

Another rotation is spent at the volleyball court. The weather determines if we use the outdoor court or the indoor 'walleyball court.'

The third rotation is held on a racquetball court, where we emphasize cooperation and teamwork."

11:30 Lunch

12:30 P.M. Field

"Each week one counselor is assigned to pick a sport or a game to work on at the field and teach it. I, for instance, work with soccer. I start with fundamentals and end with games."

2:00 Swim time

"After a hot outing at the field, there is always time for a swim. The pool is outdoors and four feet all the way across. We give them kick boards, diving rings and sticks, goggles and masks, and snorkels they can use. This is the most relaxing time of the day. The counselors have the choice of sitting and watching, or being in the pool with the kids. We always have one person in and one person out, if not more, at all times. There are no lifeguards on duty, and that is part of the reason we must be trained in CPR and first aid.

If the weather is bad, we will substitute a movie for the swim period."

3:45 Snack

4:00 Racquetball or quiet games

"At this time campers have the choice to keep the rigorous day going by choosing racquetball, or they can 'chill out' in the aerobic room and play relaxing, quiet games."

5:00 Gym

"We move all kids into the gym with all of their stuff and play another big game. Parents come between five and six to pick up their children."

SPECIAL DAYS

"On Wednesdays we usually take campers on various field trips such as a Colorado Rockies baseball game, a roller skating rink, putt-putt golf, Water World, or bowling.

The days are very busy and very exciting. There is no nap time like in some day care centers. We have great facilities to use and we take advantage of them. We make sure we always have something to do, every day of the week."

KENDALL'S HOURS

"In a normal week, I work anywhere from twenty-eight to forty hours. We have a lot of counselors, so time must be juggled between us."

THE UPSIDES AND DOWNSIDES

"The good things are the facilities. We have access to great equipment. That is one sure thing about the camp. You get what you see, and it is a nice club, so parents know that their kids are in good hands.

"The only downside about it is that for every bundle of great kids you get, there will always be a troublemaker. And that person always seems to bring others down. Naturally we are the ones responsible for taking care of that so the environment for the others is not threatened."

SALARY

"A counselor can expect to receive anywhere from minimum wage to $10 a hour. At the moment, because of my age, I am only making $5.25 per hour. The thing about it is, the hours are so good, it seems as if it makes up for little pay."

ADVICE FROM KENDALL

"One thing you must be sure of is that you are not working in a day camp or sports camp because you need money. It must be because you love kids and you're willing to deal with them and teach a lot of activities.

"If you have problems with kids, this kind of job is not for you. I guarantee, they will eat you alive."

Katherine Baum, Arts and Crafts Instructor/Cabin Counselor

In 1997, the summer before Katherine Baum started her senior year of high school, she landed her first job at Camp Conrad Weiser, a resident camp in Wernersville, Pennsylvania.

HOW KATHERINE GOT STARTED

"I got interested in camp work because I wanted to work with children. Also, I thought it would give me experience for other things, future jobs.

"I was looking in the newspaper for a summer job and this job caught my attention. It also sounded like a lot of fun."

WHAT THE JOB IS REALLY LIKE

"I work forty hours a week, eighty hours for two weeks. Because I am both an arts and crafts instructor and a cabin counselor, I don't really have much, if any, free time, so at times it can be really tiring. All the counselors are really close to one another, but because we do get tired, we can also get snappy with other counselors or the kids. We have a really good director, though, considering all the pressure she is under. And we do have a lot of fun. The hard work is worth it—the kids are always full of surprises.

"I get my kids ready in the morning and teach for the day. I teach crafts such as gimp, folk art, molding, and weaving. The thing I like most is the fact that we get paid for playing all day with kids!"

ADVICE FROM KATHERINE

"I think you should try to find a job that can make you happy, and you should be kind, and most definitely honest.

"Your salary will depend on the amount of experience you have and whether you are a counselor or a junior counselor, but you don't do it for the money."

CHAPTER 7

CAMP ADMINISTRATION

Administrative positions include camp administrator, camp director, assistant director, program director, head counselor, and trip director. Detailed definitions of these different jobs are provided in Chapter 1, but, in general, administrative jobs involve more paperwork and less interaction, if any at all, with campers.

REQUIRED QUALIFICATIONS

Administrators are expected to have had camping experience and often have come up through the ranks during summers as campers, CITs, and junior counselors. Career administrators also are expected to have bachelor's degrees, or higher, in fields related to camping, such as outdoor education, recreation, physical education, and even business administration.

Camp administrators are expected to have excellent organizational skills as well as people skills. They must be familiar with their organization's philosophy and be prepared to foster it.

Written and oral skills are a must, and more and more these days, computer skills are required.

ASSIGNMENT LENGTHS

It is more common to find camp administration jobs that are full-time. Although the arrangements will differ with each organization—from the director who lives on-site at a resident camp year-round to the administrator who is based in a city office—many top administrative positions offer permanent, secure year-round careers.

Some organizations might require their administrators to split their time between the resident or day camp during the spring and summer months and the headquarter's office during the off-season. Duties will range from hands-on programming and supervision while at camp to budgeting, recruiting, training, and policy setting in the off-season.

SALARIES FOR ADMINISTRATORS

Salaries will vary a great deal depending upon the hiring organization and its budget, the administrator's duties, and the particular position held. The range can be anywhere from $10,000 to $45,000 a year.

Fringe benefits, in addition to the usual health plans and vacation and sick leaves, can also include room and board during the camping season. Some private camps may provide opportunities to buy into the business and share profits.

CAREER ADVANCEMENT

Qualified camp administrators can move into executive positions with nonprofit agencies or become directors at larger camps. They can move up the ladder as regional or national administrators of or consultants to related associations, or become part or full owners in camps or conference centers.

FIRSTHAND ACCOUNTS

Julie Casanave, Program Director

Julie Casanave has a long history with summer camp. In 1981 she started as a camper at Camp Newfound for Girls in Harrison, Maine, then became a junior counselor in 1987. From 1988 to 1992 she was a cabin counselor; from 1990 to 1992 the head of the boat dock; in 1992 head of the Challenge Camper Program; and then in 1996 she became program director. She earned her B.A. in English in 1992 from Principia College in Elsah, Illinois.

Off-season Julie is a publications manager for a communications training company. This has kept her busy from 1992 to 1996. She was able to work out a leave of absence this past summer. Prior to 1992 she was a student and had her summers free.

HOW JULIE GOT STARTED

"Camp Newfound is an overnight summer camp for kids who go to Christian Science Sunday School. The camp runs for seven weeks. Kids come for the first three weeks, the last four weeks, or all seven weeks.

"Obviously, I just about grew up at Newfound. My interest in working there comes entirely out of my love for the place. It was a natural evolution for me to step into the counselor role after so many years as a camper. I loved what the camp experience did for me as a child, and I wanted to give back what I got. Besides, you can't really beat spending summers outside—in the sun on a lake playing with kids.

"Camps provide a remarkable opportunity for growth for kids, and being a part of it just makes me feel great. I never wonder if I'm doing something worthwhile."

BEING A PROGRAM DIRECTOR

"I was program director this past summer. That means that I was in charge of making sure everyone was having fun. My job involved making sure kids were taking the activities they wanted and that counselors were teaching them well. I was also in charge of coming up with rainy day activity ideas. I worked with the program director of the boys' camp (owned by the same people) to create and organize all-camp co-ed activities for the Fourth of July, the Olympics, weekly socials, beach parties, and other events.

"It's not bad being in charge of fun, but it's hard work. I never knew if my well-planned ideas would fly or not. There are all sorts of variables I couldn't plan for. I couldn't predict how they would affect my ideas: Would the weather cooperate? Would all the necessary equipment be available, and would it work? Would the counselors participate and lead the activities as I expected? Would the kids respond to the activities as I hoped? I never knew the answers to all these questions.

"Because of that, I had to be flexible, to be spontaneous, to lean on others, to delegate, to not feel overly responsible for making sure everyone was having a good time, and to know the difference between what I did or didn't have control over. I learned to appreciate the variables. Sometimes things worked out better than I could've anticipated."

A TYPICAL DAY

6:00 A.M. Shower, dress, spend some time getting inspired for the day. Make last-minute adjustments to today's schedule and make copies for counselors.

7:00 All-staff meeting. Director shares inspirational reading, makes announcements. I hand out revised schedule and make sure everyone knows what classes they're teaching. I remind social committee that they're meeting with the boys' social committee after fourth period to start decorating for the dance.

7:30 Flag raising, breakfast.

8:15 To main office to discuss what else needs to go into the newsletter that goes to all the parents.

9:00 Morning meeting. Everyone gathers in Lower Lodge for thirty minutes of inspirational reading, singing, and sharing of ideas. I make announcements about today: remind kids to sign up during free period to choose their next week's activities; tonight's Hawaiian luau dance with the boys.

9:45 Work out activity choices for sign-up. Make copies for everyone. Talk to counselors in charge of sign-up, and make sure they know what's expected.

11:00 Make calls about next week's entertainer. Talk to boys' program director about social: Are dinner details in place? Do the kitchen staff know what they're supposed to be doing? Write one more newsletter article.

Noon Lunch.

1:00 P.M. Rest hour (this is sacred!).

2:00 Create next week's calendar to hand out at tomorrow's staff meeting.

3:00 Talk with director about offering a softball clinic next week.

3:30 Revise sign-up choices to accommodate softball clinic. Make new copies.

4:00 Oversee sign-ups in Lower Lodge. Check out each camper as they leave the lodge.

5:00 Review master camper schedule. Is every girl signed up for something? Work out any conflicts. Advise campers and/or counselors of any changes.

6:00 Join social committee to help decorate for dance.

6:30 Dinner starts. Help kitchen staff move shish kebabs, etc., to outdoor barbecue pits.

7:45 Dance starts. Have some fun!

9:00 Begin "pucker patrol" (my favorite part of dances).

10:00 Dance ends. Start clean-up.

11:00 To bed. Make some notes about revising tomorrow afternoon's activities. It's supposed to rain.

THE UPSIDES AND DOWNSIDES

"I most like the camaraderie among staff and seeing kids have fun. I like least that there is very little down time. Also, I feel as if most of my interaction with people is business related. I rarely feel free enough to just chat with people (staff or kids)."

ADVICE FROM JULIE

"A camp job is like nothing else in the world. If you're tottering on the line about whether or not to take a camp job, do it. Do it while you're young—in high school, college, or as a recent grad. You probably won't have the energy (or schedule) for it later. The things you learn about yourself are invaluable. And the skills you develop are strong, tangible, transferable skills.

"What you'll learn at a camp about working with people and running a program will stand you in good stead wherever you end up.

"But working at a camp is not a vacation. It's a unique sort of community that fosters strong relationships and forces you to grow.

"The qualities you'll need? You should be an initiative taker. Resourceful. Someone who pays attention to and follows through on details. Someone who can make a plan and implement it or be willing to change it at the last minute. You either need to have enough energy to do it all yourself or have good powers of delegation. You also need to be willing to fail and not take it personally. Learn from it and move on."

ON GETTING A JOB

"Certainly being a camper first gives you a huge advantage when thinking about being a counselor. You can adjust to the role of counselor more quickly because you understand what the camp experience is like. You know the traditions and understand the systems.

"But it's certainly not a given that if you were a camper you'd be hired as a counselor at the same camp. There are plenty of campers I wouldn't want to see on staff! But our strongest staff members are usually the ones who have some history with us.

"In terms of whether it helps in actually getting the job, I'm not involved in the hiring process, but I can say that most of the staff had some type of camp experience before being a counselor. I can think of only three or four out of thirty who hadn't been to a camp before. I don't think that means that we've turned away people because they haven't had camp experience. I think it only means that those with camp experience are mostly the ones who apply. Usually the prospect of living with someone else's children for two months for practically no pay doesn't appeal to someone who's not been to camp before.

"I don't think not having been to a camp will preclude you from getting a counselor job. Having been to camp, however, will make your understanding of and transition to the job a bit easier. Employers will look for some kind of previous work with children. We look for people who can love kids, keep them disciplined appropriately, and teach a skill. Any concrete evidence of your attitude, creativity, and energy will help get you the job."

Tracy Larroude, Camp Director

During the school year Tracy Larroude is a classroom teacher at Hodge Elementary School in Savannah, Georgia. The camp at which she is director—Hodge Summer Computer Camp—is a two-week summer day camp, offered to all children in the Chatham County School District.

Tracy has a B.A. in recreational studies and a master's in early childhood education.

HOW TRACY GOT STARTED

"In June of 1993 I did an internship for my undergraduate degree at a camp for overweight children. I was a student intern, so it was not difficult to get the job. This is my first year working at a computer camp. I was offered this camp job by my principal. The person who ran the camp last year changed schools. I believe that I was offered the job because I have a strong knowledge of computers."

WHAT THE WORK IS LIKE

"The job is very demanding in the months before the camp and less demanding when the camp is going on. In the months before the camp, I have to hire the staff, order materials, make the brochure, and place the children into the classes. To hire the staff, I have all interested teachers write proposals of what they want to do and how they are going to utilize technology in their class.

"After hiring the teachers, I have them order what materials they need. After the classes are in order, we send the brochures to all of the elementary schools in the district. This year, we had an overwhelming response, and unfortunately we could only take about half of the applicants."

A TYPCAL DAY

"Once all of the 'hard work' is done, the actual camp work is easier. During a typical day I will go to the classes and monitor the teachers and see if they need any help with computers, printers, software, etc. I also monitor the children and make sure all of them are demonstrating good behavior. Our camp is for two weeks from 9:00 A.M. to 12:15 P.M., and many of the children do not come from our school, so we have to closely monitor them.

"I usually come in about 8:30 A.M. and leave about 1:30 P.M. The atmosphere is much more relaxed than the regular school year. The classes are smaller and the kids enjoy what they are doing on the computer—99 percent of the time!"

THE DOWNSIDES

"The downside is dealing with parents who expect the world. This is a free camp for the students, and some of our parents don't seem to appreciate what we are doing.

"Another downside is working with the staff. That was the most difficult part of running the camp for me. Most of the time they are cooperative, but there are always some who are not. I am a teacher during the school year along with them, so sometimes it is difficult to tell them what to do and what not to do.

"It is also difficult dealing with deadlines, budgets, and rules, and it is even more difficult having to relay them to peers.

"I definitely like being able to order the best materials (twelve color printers, three computers, and software), knowing that next year we will be able to use the materials in the classroom. But I dislike all the paperwork!"

ADVICE FROM TRACY

"Start early and create a database of all students, with phone numbers, addresses, classes, and other important information. This makes it much easier to access information."

THE SKILLS YOU'LL NEED

"To be the camp director of a computer camp you need to have very strong computer skills. Many problems arise with hardware, so the director needs to be familiar with basic troubleshooting. We are fortunate enough to have our computers under warranty, so there is a person who will fix problems too hard for me. For example, we had a disk stuck in a drive and a monitor that was not working. The tech came out and fixed both problems within twenty-four hours. My job is to survey the problem and fix it, if possible. And if I can't fix it, call the tech. My only problem is that we have PCs and Macs at our camp. I am a PC person so the Mac problems are difficult for me, I have to rely on another teacher to help me.

"I believe that to be a camp director you need to have very strong people skills. I talk with parents in the morning and the afternoon, and there is not a day that goes past when there is not some type of request. The purpose of our camp is to recruit children to come to our school, so I am always trying to listen and adjust to the needs of the parents and students. I believe that you have to be outgoing, friendly, happy, and confident that you have an A+ summer camp."

Scott Edgecombe, Counselor, Drama Director, Program Director

Scott Edgecombe has been working in camps in a variety of capacities for more than seven years. He earned his B.A. in English from Ontario University of Western Ontario in 1991.

HOW SCOTT GOT STARTED

"I spent seven years pursuing an acting career in Los Angeles before I found out that kids were the real reason I was put on this earth.

"I have been going to camps and working in them since 1977. I have been a CIT, a counselor, and a program director.

"I applied to be a volunteer counselor for Camp Laurel, an overnight camp for kids living with HIV/AIDS here in Los Angeles, but when they saw my experience, I was offered the program director job.

"At first I was hesitant, but I needed the money at the time. From that point I never looked back. I spent the next two years running the program for three camps and falling in love with the kids of Camp Laurel.

"This past summer I spent my first session with the camp as just a counselor. I certainly do not belittle the role by saying *just.* The week I spent with those kids changed my life, and I came back to the city, quit my acting career, and have decided to spend my life giving as many kids as possible the chance to go to camp and be a kid. In that week I changed lives forever, and in return, found my life that I had not yet realized was inside me. It's for the kids."

WHAT THE JOB IS LIKE

"I love working with kids, and this is where they get to be themselves and just have fun. For me its a chance to make new friends and be a big brother for the week. It's the only job I have ever had where I get ten times as much in return for all my work. How could you not want that all the time?

"The actual days as program director were pretty stressful for me because I let it get to me. I had to make sure everyone was where they should be for the entire week. When someone was confused, they came to me. When there were any questions, I had to guide them, and I spent most my time watching them way too closely, not trusting they could handle it on their own. From 7:00 A.M. to 1:00 A.M. each day, I was worrying about how the next hour would run. The actual camp is much harder than the paperwork!

"The upside is the kids. The downside is not getting to know them well enough because you are busy making sure they are having fun. I also hate disciplining people. The salary isn't great either, it's enough to eat, sleep, and go out once a week."

ADVICE FROM SCOTT

"You need to love what you do with all your heart. It's not a job, but a position you decide to take in a child's life. Years from now those kids will remember you; it's up to you to decide what they will remember."

CHAPTER 8

CAMP MEDICAL STAFF

All camps must provide for the medical needs of their campers and staff. Depending upon the size of the camp, it will utilize the services of just one registered nurse (RN), paramedic, or emergency medical technician (EMT), or it will hire a team of emergency medical workers headed by a medical doctor.

CAMP NURSES

Not all nurses work in hospitals or wear the traditional white uniform, in fact, approximately 32 percent of all nurses work in a setting other than a hospital. Some find employment in unusual places—on an Indian reservation, aboard a cruise ship, or lakeside at a summer camp.

RNs can enjoy their summer and earn money, too, working with children in a healthy outdoor setting at overnight or day camps. Their duties could range from simple first aid or treating insect bites to setting broken bones or teaching water safety.

The perks at a summer camp are all those the campers enjoy: fresh air, clean lakes to swim and boat in, tennis, horseback riding, and other fun activities.

Training for Nurses

At present there are four different ways you can become a registered nurse:

1. through a two-year community college, earning an associate's degree in nursing;
2. through a three-year hospital-based nursing school, earning a diploma;
3. through a four-year university program, resulting in the Bachelor's of Science Degree in nursing, or the B.S.N., as it is commonly called;
4. and, for those who already have a bachelor's degree in a different subject, there is a "generic" master's degree in nursing, a two- to three-year program beyond the bachelor's degree.

These days, and certainly in the future, the B.S.N. is being considered the minimum qualification for a satisfying career. The two-year associate's degree and the three-year hospital-based diploma programs are very quickly closing down throughout the country, and student nurses are being encouraged to enroll in four-year universities.

For many nursing specialties, it is essential to also earn a master's degree or an advanced certificate; and for some nurses, those who wish to teach, for example, a Ph.D., or doctorate, in nursing is required.

After your schooling, you will be expected to take a licensing exam for the basic RN and for any of the various specialty areas you might choose.

Salaries for Camp Nurses

Nurses working in summer camps do not expect to land the type of salaries they might in hospitals or other settings. The work is usually for a limited amount of time—two to eight weeks—and the pay can run from $1,000 to $5,000, depending on the length of the appointment.

Benefits usually include free room and board and transportation to and from the camp.

Sample Job Advertisement

To give you an example of what a job advertisement would look like, read the following: (Other sample job descriptions are provided in Chapter 3.)

> Resident camp in upstate New York is seeking an RN to work with a medical team of three nurses and one doctor. This is a co-ed camp serving 300 campers 90 miles from New York City. We offer a wide range of land and water sports, plus arts and crafts, theater, and outdoor education.
>
> Minimum age for the successful candidate is 23 years old. Salary is from $1,000 to $3,000 for 8 weeks. Start date is June 20. Room and board and transportation are provided. Contact:

CAMP PARAMEDICS AND EMTs

Some camps also hire paramedics and emergency medical technicians (EMTs) in addition to or instead of RNs. They are responsible for the basic medical needs of campers and staff.

The Role of the Emergency Medical Technician

EMTs are versed in the basics of first aid and life saving. They learn CPR, patient handling, and all the basics of medical illnesses and medical injuries.

Essentially, EMTs provide basic life-support. If an EMT and a paramedic are working together, the EMT would assist the paramedic.

If the EMT is working where higher-level paramedics are not a part of the team, he or she then would be responsible for getting the patient to the hospital.

The Role of the Paramedic

A paramedic has to be an EMT before becoming a paramedic. Paramedics are trained in very sophisticated, advanced levels of life-support. Their goal is to keep a patient alive, and they function in the field as an extension to a physician. They are the prehospital hands, eyes, and ears of the doctor and have to be able to assess a situation and react the way a doctor would.

When possible, paramedics contact the hospital and let the doctor know what they have done for the patient. Some ambulances or rescue trucks have the capability of transmitting medical data such as EKGs by radio to the hospital. At this point the doctor could let the paramedics know if there was anything else that should be done before bringing in the patient.

Paramedics have a strong relationship with physicians, who have learned over time to trust the paramedics' training and expertise.

Training for EMTs and Paramedics

EMTs can generally be trained in six to twelve weeks through a community college. During the course of their program, they spend time observing in hospitals and gaining practical experience riding with an ambulance.

To become certified, EMTs are given a practical exam through the school and a written exam through the state.

Once you have become a certified EMT, you can then go on to paramedic school. Most programs are offered through community colleges, and that is the most popular route to go, though there are a few private paramedic training schools here and there. The training for a paramedic could take anywhere from two to three semesters or two years, depending upon the state in which you live.

The course of study for a paramedic is a full curriculum with course work including anatomy, physiology, pharmacology, the administration and interpretation of electrocardiograms (EKGs), medical diagnoses, handling cardiac arrests, defibrillation, and all the related medical subjects.

Paramedic trainees spend a lot of time in hospitals learning advanced techniques. They work in operating rooms with anesthesiologists learning intubation, the process of inserting a tube into a patient's windpipe. They also spend time on hospital critical-care floors, learning from the nurses how to take care of patients. Trainees also participate in birthings and learn about pediatrics.

EMTs and paramedics also must learn about the different lifesaving equipment available to them, including extrication devices, air splints, pediatric immobilizers, suction units, portable defibrillators, and EKG machines.

In addition, to keep their certification current, emergency medical service workers must participate in continuing education classes.

Paramedics and EMTs employed at camps must love working with children and be familiar with basic water safety, rescue, and lifesaving techniques.

Salaries for Camp EMTs and Paramedics

As with most camp jobs, salaries are not glamorous. EMTs and paramedics on average earn slightly less than registered nurses.

Salaries are usually a flat fee for the summer season and include the usual fringe benefits of free housing and meals.

FIRSTHAND ACCOUNTS

Phyllis Bartram, Camp Nurse

Phyllis Bartram graduated from the University of Washington School of Nursing with a B.S. degree. She started her career in 1960, working first in public health, then as a school nurse, until she retired in 1993.

Free summers, one of the perks working with a school system, allowed Phyllis the time to work also as a camp nurse. She still spends every summer in that capacity. Currently she is the camp nurse with the Summer Enrichment Program for Talented and Gifted Students (TAG), sponsored by the College of Education, Division of Learning and Instructional Leadership of the University of Oregon in Eugene. She also has worked as the nurse for a 4-H camp and a church camp sponsored by the First Baptist Church of Eugene.

HOW PHYLLIS GOT STARTED

"I have been attracted to camp nursing largely because of my love for children. And also, when my own children were young, they were often with me at camp—as campers. I was attracted to school nursing in the first place because of being able to have my summers free with my family. Both work hand in hand together.

"I was encouraged to apply for my first camp nurse job by a nurse friend who usually worked at that camp but was unable to do so that particular year.

"As a school nurse I saw many fliers or advertisements for summer camp nursing jobs. I also saw many ads in various nursing journals and often thought that some of those would be very interesting if I had no family responsibilities.

"I have just completed my fifth summer with the Summer Enrichment Program. I first learned about this via an E-mail advertisement over our school's communication system. Because I was retiring from school nursing, I was attracted to this job as a way of 'keeping my finger in the pie' so to speak. I believe I still have something to offer the community even though I am retired."

WHAT THE WORK IS LIKE

"The Summer Enrichment Program consists of two, two-week sessions of middle school students, grades six through nine, from all over the Northwest and sometimes farther. We have had students from as far away as New York and Florida. The students live in the dorms on campus and during the day take various classes such as algebra, quantum physics, law, Shakespeare, art, poetry, psychology, etc. These are subjects that are not normally available to them at their public schools. The rest of their time consists of structured fun activities they are able to sign up for on a daily basis.

"Before camp begins, I go through the students' health forms, which were turned in with their application papers, and make note of those with special medical needs. I meet with the teachers as well as counselors and junior counselors to give a brief first-aid class and discuss student concerns.

"As the students register at the beginning of the session, I make myself available to their parents so they can give me any medications or medical instructions their children need.

CAMP NURSING DUTIES

"As the camp nurse in this program, I find my duties much the same as those in my school nursing career. The main difference is that I actually live with the kids twenty-four hours a day. My duties include:

taking care of various first aid needs;

assessing illnesses and injuries to determine when they need medical attention;

transporting students to a doctor or emergency room when I determine a need for further medical evaluation or attention;

'teaching' first aid and wellness principles during almost every encounter I have with a student;

administering prescribed medications to particular students as well as over-the-counter medications to those who have a need (Tylenol for headaches, antibiotic ointments, etc.). It is largely up to the nurse to determine whether a 'tummy ache' is due to an illness or homesickness, unhappiness with a roommate, or something else.

"I often find myself acting as Camp Mom to students and counselors alike.

"Although I am on duty twenty-four hours a day for the entire session, I carry a pager and I am able to leave campus for an occasional break. These times are taken an hour or two at a time when students are in class. I am always available, however, and return to the campus if called. I am never more than fifteen minutes away."

SOME OF THE UPSIDES

"I find that being the camp nurse is different from the other administrative jobs in that I am not viewed as an authority figure. Kids can't really get into trouble with the nurse. The counselors and other administrators often find themselves in a disciplinary role, one from which I am purposely removed. Therefore, I am not involved with patrolling the dorms to ensure the lights-out rules or other rules are being followed. Those duties are the functions of the other administrators. However, I am involved with discussions of problems and possible solutions with the administrative staff in weekly staff meetings or as problems arise.

"I love this job—just as I loved school nursing. I love young people, and it is really exciting for me to watch their development. Because I have done this for five years now, I have been able to develop relationships with certain students and staff who first arrived as sixth graders and finally 'graduate' as ninth graders. Some of these students return as junior counselors, and a few have come back as counselors or as other staff personnel. It is rewarding for me to greet old friends and develop new ones each summer.

"Another plus is that I take my sewing machine to camp with me so that I am able to use any free time finishing or starting sewing projects. I have become camp seamstress for kids as well as counselors, mending ripped seams, etc. It's not exactly a nursing function, but it is one that is appreciated by the students. That probably comes under the heading of Camp Mom.

"My salary is $2,200 for the month, plus room and board is included. It seems very adequate to me."

THE DOWNSIDES

"It is hard for me to find a downside to this job. I guess it would have to be being absent from my family for a month, although I do see them during the time I am away because I live in the same town the camp is in.

"Also, I am quite tired by the end of the month because I am up late every night, dealing with students at bedtime, and then I am up earlier than the students every morning. I am a light sleeper so I awaken easily. I have found it helpful to wear ear plugs when I do go to bed. At the end of the month I find myself catching up on sleep for most of the week following camp."

ADVICE FROM PHYLLIS

"Anyone who may be interested in camp nursing must have skill and knowledge in assessing illnesses and injuries and be able to determine when further evaluation is required. This is not always a skill held by a nurse whose experience is mainly in a clinical or hospital setting.

"A camp nurse must be able to recognize symptoms that may indicate a problem more serious than a simple cold or stomach flu. A background in schools, pediatrics, or public health, I believe, would be advantageous. A camp nurse must have an easygoing personality and, above all, love kids!"

Susan M. Burke, Camp Nurse

Susan Burke is a registered nurse with eight years experience, three as a surgical floor nurse and five as a community health nurse. The summer of 1997 was her first year as a camp nurse. She worked at Rolling Ridge United Methodist Conference Center Summer Camp, which offers a series of overnight camp programs.

HOW SUSAN GOT STARTED

"I have a Diploma in Nursing from Leominster Hospital School of Nursing in Massachusetts as well as a nearly completed B.S.N. from Fitchburg State College in Fitchburg, Massachusetts.

"I had volunteered at Rolling Ridge camp previously, and had attended camps there as a youngster. I have actually been a part of the Rolling Ridge community off and on for the last nineteen years or so—as a camper and then as a volunteer, as well as a member of the grounds crew as part of my summer jobs in high school.

"The director asked me to be their camp nurse this year. I agreed because I was looking for a change of pace and some extra money, and I also wanted to do something for Rolling Ridge."

WHAT THE CAMP IS LIKE

"The focus of the program varies from year to year, but there is always some tie-in to religion. They also go swimming, canoeing, and there is a ropes course and outdoor activities—games such as softball and other lawn games.

"The camp is in North Andover, Massachusetts, in an old estate. The building is a huge old stucco mansion that was a summer home to a wealthy family years ago. The condition is okay, and it is more camplike because of its rundown state. If ever restored to its former state, it would be comparable to one of the old Newport mansions.

"There is a dining hall and a huge kitchen from where the meals are prepped and served. The kids sleep in bunks in rooms of one, two, three, and more. It is not like camping at all. There are meeting rooms and a library. There is a pool, baseball diamond, and lawn space galore. The camp is located on a lake and is surrounded by acres of lawns and woods leading down to the lakefront. The lake is the town drinking supply, so there is no swimming other than in the pool, but they do go canoeing."

WHAT THE JOB IS LIKE

"It is fast paced at times, slow at other times, and also frustrating at times. Sometimes the lack of things to do is boring, and to me, therefore, frustrating. At times the kids arrive without the proper documentation, such as incomplete immunization records, despite their parents knowing well in advance that they are not allowed to stay without a complete health history on file and immunizations up to date.

"Sometimes parents also drop them off with prescription meds that there are no scripts for, no orders from the doctor. So I end up on the phone tracking down the parents or the doctor. If the parents say, 'Oh, it's ok, just give it to him,' I explain that I *must* have a doctor's order, that I have no license to practice medicine, only one to practice nursing.

"The kids, for the most part, though, are great fun. While there is a group of campers in the center, I work 11:00 A.M. to 7:00 P.M., Monday through Friday and for about two hours on Sunday nights after the campers arrive, to check that they have their health forms and to check any prescriptions they might have.

"I deal with the campers in relation to their medical and mental well being. My day begins with giving them their noon meds after checking with the director to see what, if anything, has gone on during the night. I then, basically, wait for something to happen.

"I give them any meds that are prescribed as prn or 'as needed' meds. These are run-of-the-mill allergy meds, inhalers, Ritalin, Zantaz. I keep an Epi pen on hand for bee stings, Benedryl, Tylenol, Motrin, Ipecac, Kaopectate, and the like.

"Some kids just have meds they take all the time, some are on antibiotics for ear infections, and there is no reason they can't come to camp with that. So, I give them what they have scripts for, as ordered by the attending doctor.

"I assess any injuries and care for them as per the standing orders we have from the medical doctor who covers the camp. I send them to the emergency room for further evaluation, if necessary. I talk to parents about injuries, or call them to come and get their child, if necessary. Then I give out any evening meds and go home. Because the camp is not far from where I live, I don't spend the nights there.

"The atmosphere is pretty laid-back. The counselors are either Methodist clergy or CITs, kids from the various churches who are old enough to help with the campers. There is a director, who lives on-site year-round with his family.

"This might sound odd, but what I like most about the work is when there is an injury. I mean that it is exciting and gives me something to do, in my capacity as an RN.

"But I also like it least when there is an injury, in that it means a child has been hurt.

"It is a very relaxed working environment and I have complete autonomy. One needs to be able to assess a situation and act accordingly. A new nurse, or a nurse without much experience, could not do this job. I could not have done the job before I was a community health nurse, which is my main job.

"But the work is kind of boring and the pay is much less, about half of what I could make working extra for the Visiting Nurses Association. I am being paid only $16.50 an hour."

ADVICE FROM SUSAN

"To be a summer camp nurse, the RN should have varied experience, should be used to working alone, should be used to making judgment calls, should be able to communicate with M.D.s well, should have excellent assessment skills, and should be used to dealing with a variety of age groups.

"A camp nurse needs to have good people skills. You should not be afraid to speak with irate parents, screaming children, and stressed M.D.s."

Rose Balasco, Camp Nurse

Rose Balasco is the head nurse at Camp Green Lane in Green Lane, Pennsylvania. It's a general activity, private co-ed camp for children, ages seven through sixteen. Rose earned her B.S.N. in 1981 from Indiana University of Pennsylvania in Indiana, Pennsylvania.

HOW ROSE GOT STARTED

"I started in camp nursing because after a car accident in 1987 I was no longer able to do hospital nursing. In 1989 I got a job at a boarding school as the weekend relief nurse through an ad in the local paper, and then when summer came, they asked me to be the day nurse for the riding camp they run.

"It was close to home so I decided to try it out, and it was okay, but the camp was not for me. I looked for a different type of camp, something less specialized. I wanted a camp with a better variety of activities so my then six-year-old daughter could have exposure to more things. I was also looking for an infirmary to work in that was better staffed and equipped. I found Camp Green Lane through an ad in a nursing journal. That was in 1991, and I have been here ever since. I had my second daughter after I started here, and she is now a camper.

"I am considering doing some school nursing after my little one is in school full-time."

WHAT THE JOB IS LIKE

"Our camp lasts for eight weeks: a few days for staff orientation at the beginning of the summer, and seven and a half weeks for the campers.

"The job of camp nurse requires a variety of experiences and skills. In a general activity camp such as Camp Green Lane, 90 percent of what we do is what I like to call 'mommy medicine.' We put Band Aids on minor wounds, give over-the-counter medications for a variety of ailments—from headaches to upset tummies to stuffy noses—and give physician prescribed medications such as the ones mom would give at home.

"Sometimes the most important medicine we give is a hug and reassurance that they will be okay. But then there are the emergencies: the asthmatic who isn't getting better in spite of her nebulizers and inhalers; the diabetic who took his insulin and then forgot his snack and now has a blood sugar of thirty; the kid who fell on his wrist playing basketball and now has no pulse; the one seizing in his cabin with no history of seizures; or the twenty-year-old carried into the infirmary with crushing chest pain but no history of cardiac trouble. These are what make the job challenging—and sometimes scary!

"We have no set hours in our infirmary. If there are no patients in the infirmary, we can close the doors and do things in camp, as long as an infirmary staff member is available for emergencies."

A TYPICAL DAY

"I am up by 8:00 A.M. and passing out medications by 8:20.

"Then it is time for breakfast. Following breakfast we have sick call with the doctor and he checks any child who wants or needs to see him. Then we are free until lunch meds.

"After lunch we may see a few more campers and give allergy shots. Then it is free again until dinner meds.

"After dinner we are free again. At night, while the kids are at evening activity, I get my medications ready for the next day. Then I pass final meds for the day and we lock the doors at 11:00 P.M.

"We do have a night buzzer for late night emergencies. If there are in-patients, we do provide any necessary care and treatment for them, and then there is always someone in the infirmary with a child—we never leave them alone."

THE UPSIDES AND DOWNSIDES

"I love the relaxed atmosphere of camp. I love the friends I have made and I love that my girls have the opportunity to attend camp. In addition to my salary, that is one of the perks. I get camp fees waived for my two children to attend as campers, plus room and board for myself and for my husband (whenever he is there).

"What I dislike is sometimes dealing with difficult parents. And there are also days when there is no doctor available, and I feel as if I have to be both doctor and nurse."

CHAPTER 9

KITCHEN STAFF

Camp jobs are not just limited to counselor, nursing, or administrative positions. All overnight camps and some day camps have kitchen and dining facilities and need qualified people to staff them.

Jobs titles run the gamut from experienced food service managers and chefs to cooks and kitchen aids earning extra money working in summer jobs.

FOOD SERVICE MANAGERS

In camps and other food service facilities that operate long hours, seven days a week, the manager is aided by several assistant managers, each of whom supervises a shift of workers.

At some camps managers interview, hire, and, when necessary, discharge workers. They familiarize newly hired workers with the camp's policies and practices and oversee their training. Managers also schedule the work hours and days off of employees.

Food service managers supervise the kitchen and the dining room. They oversee food preparation and cooking, checking the quality of the food and the sizes of portions to ensure that dishes are prepared correctly and in a timely manner. Some kitchen managers

97

must order supplies and maintain records of the costs of supplies and other equipment.

If a staff member is out sick, managers may roll up their sleeves and help with the cooking, clearing of tables, or other tasks. They direct the cleaning of the kitchen and dining areas and the washing of tableware, kitchen utensils, and equipment to maintain camp and government sanitation standards. They also monitor workers on a continual basis to ensure compliance with health and safety standards and other local regulations.

Managers are among the first to arrive at work and the last to leave at night. They also are responsible for locking up, checking that ovens, grills, and lights are off.

COOKS

Head cooks and their assistants are responsible for preparing meals that are tasty and attractively presented. Chefs are the most highly skilled, trained, and experienced kitchen workers. Although the terms *chef* and *cook* are still sometimes used interchangeably, cooks generally have more limited skills. Many chefs have earned fame for both themselves and the restaurants, hotels, and institutions where they work because of their skill in artfully preparing the traditional favorites and in creating new dishes and improving familiar ones.

COOK HELPERS/KITCHEN WORKERS

Other helpers, under the direction of managers and cooks, perform tasks requiring less skill. They weigh and measure ingredients; fetch pots and pans; clean, peel, and slice potatoes, other vegetables, and fruits; and make salads. They also may do some baking or cut and grind meats, poultry, and seafood in preparation for cooking. Such helpers are responsible for general kitchen cleaning, including cleaning of utensils, dishes and silverware, equipment, counters, and floors.

The number and types of workers employed in camp kitchens depend on the size of the camp and the number of people it feeds.

DINING ROOM STAFF

At some camps the tasks of setting the tables, serving the food, filling salt and pepper shakers, clearing the tables, and mopping the floors after meals fall to senior campers or CITs. Other camps hire dining room staff to take care of those duties. Dining room staff usually work split shifts.

WORKING CONDITIONS

While counselors and other staff get a chance to participate in camp activities, kitchen workers seldom, if ever, get the same opportunities. They might, however, get to use the pool or take a swim during times when the campers aren't using the facilities—early in the morning or late at night, for example, or during scheduled camper rest periods.

The day begins early for kitchen workers and runs late. Meals are generally served three times a day, and the food needs to be prepared and the kitchen kept clean and organized throughout the day.

After breakfast most kitchen staff spend the rest of the morning preparing for lunch. Sometimes, between the lunch and dinner hours, a kitchen worker might be given a break for an hour or two.

If a camp has late evening activities or offers afternoon snacks, the kitchen staff has to be on duty. When campers are taken on field trips, often the kitchen staff is responsible for preparing boxed or bagged lunches for each camper and staff member.

TRAINING FOR KITCHEN STAFF

Food Service Management

Many food service manager positions are filled by promoting experienced kitchen staff and service workers who have demonstrated potential for handling increased responsibility.

A bachelor's degree in restaurant and food service management provides a particularly strong preparation for a career in this occupation in a variety of settings, including restaurant work.

In 1997 more than 160 colleges and universities offered four-year programs in restaurant and hotel management or institutional food service management. For persons who do not want to pursue a four-year degree, a good alternative is provided by the more than eight-hundred community and junior colleges, technical institutes, and other institutions that offer programs in these fields leading to an associate degree or other formal award below the bachelor's degree.

Both two-year and four-year programs give instruction in subjects such as accounting, business law and management, food planning and preparation, and nutrition. Some programs combine classroom and laboratory study with internships that provide on-the-job experience.

Cooks

An increasing number of cooks are obtaining their training through high school or post–high school vocational programs and two- or four-year colleges. Cooks also may be trained in apprenticeship programs offered by professional culinary institutes, industry associations, and trade unions. An example is the three-year apprenticeship program administered by local chapters of the American Culinary Federation in cooperation with local employers and junior colleges or vocational education institutions. In addition, some camps provide their own training for cooks. People who have had courses in commercial food preparation may be able to start as a cook without first having to spend time in a lower-skilled kitchen job.

Some vocational programs in high schools offer this kind of training, but usually these courses are given by trade schools, vocational centers, colleges, professional associations, and trade unions. Postsecondary courses range from a few months to two years or more and are open in some cases only to high school graduates. The armed forces also are a good source of training and experience.

Although curricula may vary, students usually spend most of their time learning to prepare food through actual practice. They learn to bake, broil, and otherwise prepare food, and to use and care for kitchen equipment. Training programs often include courses in planning menus, determining portion size and food cost control, purchasing food supplies in quantity, selecting and storing food, and using leftover food to minimize waste. Students also learn public health rules for handling food. Training in supervisory and management skills sometimes is emphasized in courses offered by private vocational schools, professional associations, and university programs.

Culinary courses are given by 550 schools across the nation. The American Culinary Federation accredited seventy of these programs in 1993. Accreditation is an indication that a culinary program meets recognized standards regarding course content, facilities, and quality of instruction. The American Culinary Federation has only been accrediting culinary programs for a relatively short time, however, and many programs have not yet sought accreditation.

Kitchen Workers

Some kitchen staff have had previous experience working in restaurants or fast-food establishments. Kitchen staff jobs do not usually require any specific educational qualifications, and most workers are taught their skills on the job.

JOB OUTLOOK

The job outlook is excellent for cooks and other kitchen workers. There is usually a high turnover rate in this area because jobs are seasonal and are often filled by students earning money to see themselves through school.

Workers under the age of twenty-five have traditionally filled a significant proportion of the lesser skilled jobs in this occupation. The pool of young workers is expected to continue to shrink through the 1990s, but then begin to grow. Many employers will be forced to offer higher wages, better benefits, and more training to attract and retain workers in these jobs.

SALARIES

Earnings of food service managers vary greatly according to their responsibilities and the type and size of establishment. Based on a survey conducted for the National Restaurant Association, the median base salary of managers in restaurants was estimated to be about $27,900 a year in early 1993, but managers of the largest restaurants and institutional food service facilities often had annual salaries in excess of $45,000.

Wages of cooks and other kitchen and dining room workers vary depending on the size of the camp and its budget. Many earn an hourly wage from $5 to $7 an hour. Some are paid a flat fee, and this can range from $1,000 to $5,000 or more, depending upon the length of the season.

FIRSTHAND ACCOUNTS

Diane Boone, Director of Food Service

Now retired, Diane Boone worked for twenty-four years in a variety of camps in the San Bernardino Mountains of southern California. At varying times she held positions as cook's helper, head cook, food service manager, and food service director. She also worked as a cook with the sheriff's department.

Diane also owned a business called Boone's Cooking Service, which provided food service to camps used as conference centers in the winter months.

HOW DIANE GOT STARTED

"I needed a job. We had just moved to the mountains and I heard about the job opening at Thousand Pines Baptist Camp. Because I had restaurant experience I applied. I started off as a cook's helper.

"It was also my love for children that attracted me to the idea of working in camps. And my love for cooking. This is a wonderful 'service' profession.

"I also loved nature, and this was a very rewarding job, making the camp experience better by providing good home-style cooking."

WHAT THE JOB IS REALLY LIKE

"Most of the camps I worked in had a capacity of up to five-hundred. I would not say 'relaxed' is a word often used to describe a camp cook. I have not met a relaxed cook yet. I would have to say the unexpected is the rule for a camp cook. You had better be flexible and ready to change menus at a moment's notice and be a good sport about it.

"'Interesting' best describes life in camp, especially in the kitchen. We are 'Mom,' counselor, first-aid person—and that is just what we do in our 'spare' time! We deal with troubled kids (why do you think the parents wanted their children to attend at a good wholesome camp for the summer?), natural disasters, shorted food deliveries, angry camp directors, and upset staff (often other than our own kitchen staff). My duties include planning menus; interviewing, hiring, training, and scheduling staff; ensuring sanitation and the safe handling of food; actually preparing food; taking inventory and ordering all kitchen supplies; organizing the pantry and walk-in freezer; and overseeing the daily on-site cooking of main entrees.

I am also responsible for keeping a full pantry. I found I needed at least two weeks worth of meals in my pantry at all times in order to be prepared for those inevitable emergencies: roads wash out in summer rains, camp buses break down on the way up the hill, vendors back-order items you need—so you'd better have good back up.

"I always keep some powdered milk on hand in case the milk doesn't come in. There are no stores to run to in the wilderness areas. I have had to make my own mayonnaise on more than one occasion. Many times I make my own bread products because the deliveries don't come in.

"Power outages are common in the high country, too. I worked one camp where it had a beautiful, modern, stainless steel kitchen—all electric. Almost every afternoon my power was off because of daily thunderstorms. I quickly learned to have my dinner meal ready by noon and placed on the heavy steel plates on top of my ranges. There the meal stayed above 160 degrees F. until dinner at 5:00 P.M.

"I also learned to keep a supply of paper products on hand for when the dishwasher broke down or the power was off.

"Also, keeping big pots of boiling water on the stove was a must for pot washing later.

"Camp directors for summer camps often know nothing about food service. You have to learn to be a politician real fast, and also to be flexible. Sometimes I have had to go along with something I know won't work just because the director ordered me to; then you have to help them save face when it falls apart.

"I also learned early in my career to make friends with the wild creatures I shared the beautiful locations with. I have lots of fun bear stories. Fortunately, I never met a black bear I could not be friends with. I learned to talk, whistle, or sing when I left the camp kitchen and headed for my quarters so the bear would know it was me and not be scared. Only frightened or startled bears cause any problems.

"Raccoons also visited me every night in most camps. I let my staff and sometimes a camper feed them raw eggs. Skunks, too, were common as well as yellow jackets (a can of grease set some distance from the serving area drew them away from the campers), snakes, mice, and wood rats."

A TYPICAL DAY

4:00 A.M. Rise and shine.

5:00 Open kitchen, start dishwasher and coffee pots, boil water for hot cereal, place bacon in oven, turn warmers on.

5:30 Have a coffee break and evaluate the day's menus and staffing.

6:00 Helpers arrive.

6:00–7:30 Get breakfast cooked.

8:00 Serve breakfast.

8:30 Staff breakfast break.

9:00 Cleanup and begin lunch preparation, perhaps getting sack lunches ready for field trips.

10:30–11:00 Do my inventory check and make out food orders.

11:00 Finalize lunch preparation.

Noon Serve lunch.

12:30 P.M. Staff lunch break.

1:00 Clean up.

1:00–3:00 Start dinner and deal with any vendors.

3:00–4:00 Take a break if I can.

4:00–5:00 Make final dinner preparations.

5:00 Serve dinner.

5:30 Staff dinner break.

6:00 Clean up and prepare evening snack for camp counselors.

"With luck, I get to leave at this point, if I have a reliable assistant cook to supervise clean up and prep for the next morning."

ACCOMMODATIONS

"I have stayed in tents, Quonset huts, nice nurses' quarters, my own camper, and even commuted to nearby camps.

"Room and board for me and my two daughters and meals for my husband were always a part of my negotiations for any job. In fact, every summer my husband would usually come and stay two weeks of his vacation at whatever camp I was in."

THE UPSIDES AND DOWNSIDES

"I loved my work. I loved the challenge, the adventure, the surprises, the wonderful children and adults I met. I loved the friends I made along the way during twenty-four years of working with young people. My staff all became my 'adopted' children. You should see the pile of Christmas cards and letters I get each year. It is wonderful and so fulfilling. I am so glad I chose to be a camp cook all those years. I have dear former staff members I have seen grow up and now have families of their own. I've seen some of my 'kids' grow up to become forest rangers, doctors, counselors, and missionaries.

"I loved all those evenings when staff would come into my kitchen late at night and help me crack fifty dozen eggs for the morning—the crazy, fun, egg-cracking contests in the middle of the night; the star walks; the meteor shower watches; the camp fires; the camaraderie; the flooded kitchens; the rats loose in the walk-in; the bread dough that 'grew' and crawled across the kitchen floor during dinner break; the 'Christmas in July' parties; and all the cookouts.

"I think some of my favorite times have been with the bears. I have met many a bear late at night after I have closed up the kitchen. I love the fact that most camps are in the most beautiful locations you can imagine. I have worked at camps at 8,500 feet with a lake and wild donkeys. I have worked at camps at 7,500 feet with beautiful meadows that become gorgeous lakes as the winter snows melted, and that we could canoe on by the end of summer.

"I have also worked many adult conferences and enjoyed their speakers and the fellowship.

"The downside…if you are not a 'giver,' if you need instant gratification, if you must be concise and live on an even keel, then don't even think of becoming a camp cook.

"And honestly? It can be a thankless job sometimes. It seems people just have to complain about something, and we often get it. Every one but the kitchen staff gets to go to campfires and other activities, but we have to work to get ready for the next day.

"One problem we face today in food service is the fact that this is a generation of 'fast food' addicts. If our macaroni and cheese doesn't look exactly like the Kraft product, look out! The kids, and even the adults, want no unfamiliar foods. We have had to become very creative in coming up with foods they will eat. Pizza and outdoor barbecues work well.

"We work long hard hours. The old saying—we are overworked and underpaid—is just how it is."

SALARIES

"If money is the only reason someone wants to be a camp cook, then think again. The most rewarding 'wage' I received was the satisfaction of a job well done. I helped make the campers' experience better because they were well fed with tasty meals.

"The best salary I ever got in camp was $7.50 an hour in 1988, and I was the head cook. Most get little more than minimum wage plus meals. To contrast, when I was a cook with the sheriff's department, I made $15.50 an hour plus fantastic benefits. But, I must say the camp experience got me the sheriff job."

ADVICE FROM DIANE

"If you have a cheerful disposition, a gentle spirit, the patience to handle unexpected situations, and a willingness to keep on learning, then you are a candidate for a successful career in 'camping.'

"As far as cooking goes, buy a cookbook that covers cooking for fifty. Trust me on this one! I have worn out three editions in my thirty-four years of being a professional institutional cook.

"I became a food service director because the food service director at the camp where I was working as assistant cook had a heart attack. She gave me her old *Food for Fifty* cookbook and told me everything I would need to know to run the kitchen was in it.

She was right, and that was the start of a great career. (See Appendix B for more information on this book.)

"I would also recommend some courses in food handling, going to restaurant shows, watching cooking shows on TV (I've gotten lots of little shortcuts from the experts this way), and taking any classes offered by local colleges (some are free) that deal with cooking and general cooking skills. Camps are hard up for dedicated and qualified staff.

"You must also have some skills in baking from scratch, vendor management, people management, sanitation control, and good home-style cooking.

"A final word: I would not trade my years as a camp cook for any amount of money. It was a hard life, but the rewards were worth it to me and my family."

Jonathan Werner, Camp Cook

Jonathan Werner is a high school student who spends part of his summer as a cook at Camp UTADA, a program for children with diabetes.

HOW JONATHAN GOT STARTED

"I started eleven years ago as a camper, when I was told I had diabetes. My doctor recommended that I go to camp. I started working in the camp in the program area, where we played games and had different activities.

"Just this past summer I worked in the kitchen, and I will work there again in two weeks. I got the job by talking to the camp director. He passed me along to the food service manager, who told me which camp sessions I would be attending (there are seven sessions during the summer, a week each) and what I would be doing."

WHAT THE JOB IS REALLY LIKE

"As a cook I wake up at 6:00 A.M. and start breakfast. It takes a long time to cook for sixteen families! (There are three family sessions and four other sessions for older campers.)

"I get done cooking as the families come in to eat. We get them seconds, if they need them, then we clean up breakfast and start lunch. We do the same thing, then start dinner.

"It is really fun. What I like most is being involved in camp and spending time with friends and others with diabetes.

"All the jobs at camp are volunteer except the kitchen."

ADVICE FROM JONATHAN

"I would advise everyone wanting to work in the kitchen to get plenty of rest! Don't plan on just lying around. Get your work done fast, so you have time to play after the work is done. Be a really hard worker, and if you like it, then you will probably be asked to come back again."

Rose Elizabeth Ledbetter, Dining Room Staff

Rose Elizabeth Ledbetter has worked in camps in a variety of roles. She is currently a student at Jacksonville State University in Alabama, working toward a B.A. in English. (Her experiences as a lifeguard are detailed in Chapter 6.)

HOW ROSE ELIZABETH GOT STARTED

"I was fourteen, so, of course the most attractive aspect of working at the camp was being away from home. For us, it was as if we were out on our own. Most of the children at camp were a great deal younger than we were, and though there were some who were our age, we felt vastly superior because we had no one telling us what to do. It was also about the only job available for someone my age.

"I got the job because a friend was going to be working at the camp. Her parents were friends with the director.

WORKING IN THE DINING ROOM

"I started out as kitchen help, the lowest of the low. Before each meal we set up trays, drinks, silverware, glasses, napkins, chaffing dishes for the buffet, and anything else that might need to be set up. While the campers ate, we filled drinks, refilled the buffet, and cleared trash. After the meal we washed dishes, swept and cleaned the dining room, took out the trash, and hosed down the kitchen floor.

"Once a week we waxed the dining room floor and every two weeks, as campers left, we helped the woman in charge of the kitchen take an inventory."

ACCOMMODATIONS

"Looking back now, I realize this was really hard work, but at the time, I was in heaven. I was free to do what I wanted as long as I turned up for work on time. We were housed in the upstairs of the camp director's residence with our own separate entrance. So we really were on our own. There were four large rooms, each with its own bathroom and two beds, and one large common area furnished with couches and chairs that had been cast off from the cabins. Some of them must have dated back to the sixties, judging from the lovely shades of lime green and orange they were uphol-stered in."

SNACK BAR WORK

"That summer was awesome, and although, by Alabama law, I was old enough to get a 'real job' the next year, I went back to camp. That summer I still worked in the dining room for set ups, but after the meals, instead of cleanup, I left to set up the snack bar where the children could buy snacks and colas after their afternoon recreation. To earn a pay hike that summer, I also helped clean the cabins after each group left every two weeks or so and helped stock and prepare the cabins when a new group was coming in. We also cleaned the bathrooms and the bunk area."

A TYPICAL DAY

"A typical day when I first started camp began at 6:00 in the morning. At this time I worked in the dining hall. Breakfast for the campers started at 7:00 A.M., so we had to have everything ready for the campers and then feed ourselves and the other staff before the campers came into the dining hall.

"Depending on how many cabins were full and how many groups we had that week, breakfast could last from thirty minutes to an hour and a half. When the meal was done, we began our cleanup. The buffet came down and those dishes were left to soak for the cook to clean. The campers dumped and stacked their own trays and glasses, so we simply picked them from the stacks and washed them. When the kitchen was clean, we swept the dining room and dumped the trash out back in the dumpsters. Usually one of the guys helped us with that because the trash was too heavy for us.

"There were two boys who lived at the camp year-round, Cambodian refugees the camp directors had taken in. One day one of them was helping us dump the trash. He was sticking his hands into the trash cans of grits, eggs, biscuits, and other scraps and pretending to eat it. We laughed and laughed. Suddenly he sobered and looked at his hands. 'I used to have to eat like this,' he said. I will never forget his face.

"Sometimes we had other duties: cleaning windows, sweeping the porches, hosing off the back loading dock, stocking supplies. There were several of us on the kitchen staff, so the work was divided and went quickly. Then we were free until 11:30 to begin setting up for lunch. We repeated the same process for lunch and for dinner.

"Sometimes the campers had wienie roasts or they grilled at their cabins for dinner, and that meant we were free to do what we wanted. We did the same things the other campers did. We hiked, swam, and canoed. Unlike the campers, we had radios and TVs in our rooms and we used them, too. I remember one British chaperone who came with a group. She found out that we had a TV and she stayed up until the wee hours of the morning, hidden in our rooms, so that she could watch the wedding of Charles and Di live on TV.

"At this camp, like at most others, you often do double duty. It is sort of like living at home; if something needs to be done, you just do it."

THE UPSIDES AND DOWNSIDES

"I suppose what I liked the most about the job the first few years was the freedom. No one told us a bedtime or what we could do or when we could do it. For a fourteen-year-old that freedom was heaven.

"After that, the best thing was the friendship. Most of the workers returned year after year, so we were a very tight-knit group. We were best friends. We also did our share of kissing and taking 'nature walks' with the boys who worked at the camp. Camp always seemed more like fun than work, even when I was cleaning toilets.

"Now, what I appreciate about the camp was what it taught me. The last two years of camp we had cancer victims there. Those children taught me more about life than any other single thing I have ever experienced. They helped heal the wounds of my own mother's death. They taught me about courage and spirit and living."

ADVICE FROM ROSE ELIZABETH

"Finding a job at a camp will probably be easy. If you are a churchgoer, your minister can provide you with a list of camps in the state run by churches. The YMCA has summer camps all over the country, including sleep-over and day camps. Contact your local YMCA for information. Look in the backs of magazines such as *Teen* and *Seventeen.* The same camps that advertise for campers also need staffers. Just call the number in the ad and ask for an application for employment.

"There are several Girl Scout camps in every state. Look in your Yellow Pages under Girl Scout Council. However, most Girl Scout camps look for staffers who are seventeen and older.

"Remember that while the pay may not seem as high as that for some other summer jobs, room and board are included in most salaries. Also remember that even if the pay is lower, you have little to spend your money on at a camp, and you'll have a lot left over at the end of the summer. It is a great way to save.

"The qualities you'll need to work at a camp are the same as they are for many jobs. Most important is a willingness to work. The pranks and fun you see in movies such as *Meatballs,* for example, are very close to real life in a camp, but those movies don't show the hard work. Remember, you aren't there as a camper, you are staff and you are getting paid. Be flexible. If you are willing to take on other tasks, even if they aren't in your job description, you may be able to move up. If you have special skills, you might find a camp to match them. These days there are camps for everything from music and writing to skateboarding and survival skills."

Katie Krieck, Assistant Cook

Katie Krieck has been working at camps for the past six summers as a counselor and as an assistant cook. The last three seasons she has been at Camp Boyhaven, a Cub Scout overnight camp in Middlegrove, New York. Currently she attends Bentley College in Waltham, Massachusetts.

HOW KATIE GOT HER JOB

"I have no official training for this job. I am an English major and I work for the Marriot food service at my school. I have been at this camp for three years, and I learned all I know from my first summer as a prep cook. My bosses that year, who were my age, taught me all I know.

"I started to work in camp because I love working with kids, but I took the kitchen position rather than a program position because I am a very shy person and don't deal well with meeting new people. With the number of people that go through the camps, I would have probably panicked. I like being able to see the kids and interact with them when I feel comfortable.

"The first job I got in a camp was a favor for a friend. It wasn't a kitchen staff position, I was a floating counselor. She was in a bind and needed counselors. She fudged some paperwork because I wasn't quite 'of age' at the time, and then, I was in.

"That same person recommended me for my current job. She works for the council and knew the camp director that year. That got me through the first year. Since then, I was given the job because the people who ran the camp and did the hiring knew me and trusted my capabilities. They knew how much I loved Camp Boyhaven, the kids, and the kitchen."

WHAT THE WORK IS REALLY LIKE

"My duties include everything from planning the meal, to prepping it, to preparing the main courses, to serving them—and, then, finally cleaning up and sometimes pitching in with the dishes.

"I am to keep the kitchen in clean, working order and make sure the rest of staff members do their job. This is no easy task considering the 'help' is a group of fifteen- and sixteen-year olds who have very little to no work ethic. I have to clean up and finish up what they don't finish—as well as do my job.

"The summer is long and tiring. Last summer we went through two head cooks because the first one messed up badly. This summer the head cook is older and she can't lift things most of the time, leaving it to me to pick up the pieces. Our staff this summer has also dropped from eight to three. One quit, one was moved, one was hurt, one left on vacation, and one was a CIT volunteer who had to leave."

A TYPICAL DAY

"My day starts at 5:30 A.M. I get up and shower and unlock the doors of the kitchen by 5:45. My prep cook lights the grills at 6:00 and by 6:30 we have to make whatever we're having for breakfast, maybe pancakes or French toast.

"It is far from boring; it is always extremely hectic. You cannot end one thing without thinking about what you have to do next. Many times I would find myself going to bed at night and worrying about dinner for the next day. The normal tasks always had to be done, like prepping our salad bar and making up bowls of peanut butter and jelly, as well as getting the main course done. This is no easy task when you have several sixteen-year-olds whining about when they could get a break and your head cook complaining about how much she is hurting. It is very frustrating and nerve-racking—especially for someone like me who hasn't really experienced this much pressure before. I am almost twenty and I feel about thirty as I wind up this summer. A lot of weight is put on your shoulders."

THE UPSIDES

"I love the kids—they are so cute and they do talk to you, even in the kitchen. Especially if you go out to the program areas, they get a kick out of swimming with the cook or talking to the person who cooks the food for them.

"I remember last summer I would go out and see my friend who was director of scout skills. The kids would start talking to me, and they seemed to be interested in the fact that the person who cooks for them is like their older sister, or their babysitter—not a seventy-five-year-old bearded women.

"I also enjoy the people I meet. The leaders come in and chat. They are impressed when they find out how old I am and how much I have to do.

"The leader commended us by saying, 'I know how hard it is to cook for a family of four—I could only imagine one-hundred screaming kids. Good job.' I loved that because it is how I think.

"I love cooking—plain and simple. I get very offended when people pick on how I cook."

THE DOWNSIDES

"I absolutely hate the complaints. We get them all the time, and they are very insulting to my ego. I get aggravated—especially when the staff complains. I do everything within my power to make the food taste good, and all they do is complain.

"The hassles of getting the food out on time and hot is another big problem. Keeping the food hot is key—because if it is, we get less complaining.

"The kids and adults can be very picky—even the staff gets to be a pain. I try to cater to them specially, to keep them healthy and happy."

SALARIES

"The way Boyhaven works your pay depends on how many years you have been there, how old you are, and what your position is. I made $200 last year and $225 this year. It was low for the work I did, and there were many arguments about it, but something other than the salary kept me there."

ADVICE FROM KATIE

"You need to have nerves of steel. This is a must! You need them to deal with other crew members and the problems and the annoyances that come with everything that happens.

"Another thing is to love the camp you work at and have spirit—camp spirit and scout spirit, if it happens to be a scout camp like mine. I had both and it was hard to be one of the only ones with it. It will help you survive, however, and the love for the place and kids and the spirit will help you stay where you are and not quit despite any difficulties you face.

"Also, try to keep some sort of sense of humor and stand tall. Keep your head up high no matter what, and keep smiling. Never quit, it'll all be worth it.

"I just got home from camp and let me tell you that after a day or two of sleep, I will be missing it—missing my friends and the feeling of independence. So when you are there, relish every minute of it. You'll regret it if you don't."

CHAPTER 10

RELATED RECREATIONAL SETTINGS AND EMPLOYMENT

In addition to summer camps, there are a variety of settings that offer related employment. Although summer camp work is, by its very nature, seasonal, recreation workers in other settings can pursue full-time careers that bring in higher incomes and offer year-round benefits. The details of working conditions, salaries, and training requirements are discussed in Chapters 1 and 2. This chapter will give you a look at the different settings open to you and give you some firsthand accounts of what the work is actually like.

SETTINGS FOR RECREATION WORKERS

Private Industry

Large companies often employ recreation workers at the workplace to organize and direct leisure activities and athletic programs for employees and their families. Activities could include bowling and softball leagues, social functions, travel programs, discount services, and, to an increasing extent, exercise and fitness programs. These activities are generally for adults.

Any openings would be listed in the help wanted ads or made known through the company's personnel office. Some companies also might list openings with private and/or state employment agencies or in newsletters put out by related professional associations.

Cruise Ships

Cruise ships offer employment for social directors that is very similar to the role of camp counselors. An in-depth look at this career is provided for you later in this chapter, with details on duties, salaries, getting started, and a firsthand account from an assistant cruise director. See detailed information on working as a cruise staff member later in this chapter.

Playgrounds and City Recreation Areas

City playgrounds, parks, community pools, civic centers, and community centers offer both full-time, year-round and part-time, summer employment for trained recreation workers, youth leaders, lifeguards, swim instructors, sports directors, fitness instructors, and counselors. Look through your local White Pages to find city and community center listings; then telephone to ask for the proper procedure for job applications.

Health Clubs

Health clubs hire a variety of trained fitness instructors, personal trainers, and sports directors to service both adults and children.

To meet safety standards and insurance and state and local regulations, most health club–type settings require that their instructors and trainers have appropriate qualifications or licenses.

Personal trainers hold a great deal of responsibility for their clients' welfare and must be fully trained in what they do.

There are a few routes trainers can take to learn their craft and become certified. Some universities offer exercise science or exercise physiology programs. You also can do a home study through the American Council on Exercise (ACE), then sit for the exam they give twice a year.

The American College of Sports Medicine (ACSM) is also a certifying body. Both tests have written and practical components.

The practical component of each test consists of sub-max testing, where you are evaluated while you monitor a client's heart rate and blood pressure. You also will put your client through a workout, and your spotting techniques and how you interact will be judged. Once you have become a personal trainer you'll need continuing education credits to keep up your certification.

A training program can take two weeks, eight weeks, or four years, if you pursue a bachelor's degree.

Personal trainers in a health club can work on commission or on an hourly rate, earning anywhere from $45 to $150 an hour, depending upon the budget of the clientele.

Personal trainers can set their own hours. If they choose, they can train only four people in a day and be done. But if self-employed, personal trainers have taxes and insurance expenses to consider, and they may choose to take on more clients.

A firsthand account of work as a personal trainer is provided for you later in this chapter.

Theme Parks and Tourist Attractions

Theme parks and tourist attractions offer employment for activity directors, tour guides, presenters, and other related positions to service both adult and children visitors. Contact the personnel office of the theme park or attraction that interests you.

Churches and Synagogues

Church- and synagogue-sponsored organizations such as the Christian Youth Organization (CYO) or Jewish Community Centers (JCCs) have a need for part-time and full-time youth leaders and other related recreation workers with varied backgrounds and training. Contact directly the particular church or temple group for which you are interested in working. A firsthand account of a church group youth leader is provided for you later in this chapter.

YMCAs

The YMCA is one of the biggest employers of youth leaders, recreation workers, activity and speciality instructors, and other related positions. Jobs are filled both in YMCA city and town centers as well as at a variety of Y-sponsored resident and day camps around the country. Contact your local Y for information on job openings and requirements.

Museums

Museums and planetariums—those catering to adults as well as children's museums and discovery centers—provide special activities for children in year-round, summer, and after-school programs. Jobs in this category usually fall under the auspices of the education or interpretation departments.

The American Association of Museums (AAM) puts out a monthly newsletter called *Aviso.* At least half of each issue is devoted to listings for employment opportunities and internships. See Appendix A for the AAM's address.

Salaries vary widely from position to position, but are generally low, as are most pay scales for education-related fields.

How you proceed with your training will depend upon your interests and circumstances. If you are clear from the start what avenue you wish to pursue, you can tailor-make a course of study for yourself at the university of your choosing.

Traditionally new hirees to the field of museum work have completed at least a bachelor's and often a master's degree in an academic discipline appropriate to the intended career. Those wishing to pursue education or interpretation positions can enroll in specific museum studies programs or work toward a degree in related areas of education or public relations.

The American Association of Museums publishes the *Guide to Museum Studies & Training in the United States,* which lists more than eighty museum studies programs offering undergraduate or graduate courses or both. Most of these programs came into existence after 1975, and many new programs continue to join the ranks each year.

Zoos

Similarly to museums, zoos offer special activities and programs geared toward children. These programs are generally scheduled year-round and offer both full- or part-time employment.

Competition is keen for employment within zoos, and the more qualifications you have the better. Most zoos require at least a bachelor's degree combined with hands-on experience. Internships and volunteering are excellent ways to gain that experience. Later in this chapter is a firsthand account from a zoo volunteer.

CLOSE-UP LOOK AT CRUISE STAFF WORK

Probably everyone, at one time or another, has seen reruns of *The Love Boat* on television and watched Julie, Doc, Isaac, Gopher, and Captain Steubing go about their daily activities, interacting with and making sure that passengers have the best vacations of their lives.

Although the reality might not exactly mirror life on the popular series, being part of a cruise ship staff can be fun and exciting, with the opportunity to travel to exotic ports, meet all different kinds of people, make new friends, and lead a carefree lifestyle.

Cruise lines employ all sorts of personnel to handle the many tasks involved with running a ship. Of most interest to those considering a career in recreation would be what is called "cruise staff," another term for social or activities director or assistant cruise director. Job titles and responsibilities vary from ship to ship, but in many ways, the work of the cruise staff is similar to a counselor position at a summer camp.

What It's Like to Be Part of a Cruise Staff

Although filled with its share of excitement and glamour, working on a ship involves a lot of hard work. Cruise staff put in long hours—anywhere from eight to fifteen hours a day, seven days a week—and must maintain a high level of energy and always be cordial and friendly to passengers.

Cruise staff members are generally involved with organizing activities, games, and social events, including shuffleboard and ring toss, Bingo, aerobics classes, basketball, golf putting (and driving—off the stern of the ship), and pool games. They also participate in cocktail parties and masquerade balls and take every opportunity to make sure passengers feel comfortable and are enjoying themselves.

Many of the cruise staff also double as entertainers and need to have some talent for performing, whether as singers, musicians, or DJs.

When in port, most of the crew is allowed to go ashore and have time off to explore, although some cruise staff function as chaperones, helping passengers find their way around foreign locales.

Activities onboard ship usually follow a rigid schedule, with little time in between for the crew to rest or take a break. With a constant eye on their watches, cruise staff run from one activity to another, announcing games over the loudspeaker, setting up the deck for exercise classes, supervising ring toss tournaments or other special events, and encouraging everyone to participate.

An outgoing, energetic individual would be in his or her element in such a job; someone who lacks those skills would find the work very difficult.

Salaries and Benefits

Although salaries are not overly generous, the additional benefits are. Cruise staff are provided with free housing while onboard ship and all they can eat. It's not necessary for a full-time employee of a cruise line to maintain quarters ashore and, therefore, most of the salary can be saved.

Getting Started in Cruise Recreation

A college education is not necessary, but some cruise lines prefer to see an applicant with a degree in psychology, hotel management, physical education, recreation, or communications. It's also a good idea to know another language, especially Spanish or German.

Even more important are the following personal qualities a good cruise staff member should possess: patience, diplomacy, tolerance for a wide variety of people, a never-ending supply of energy, an outgoing and genuinely friendly nature, enthusiasm, artistic talent, and athletic ability.

Most successful applicants land their jobs by applying directly to the various cruise lines, which are located mainly in Miami, Fort Lauderdale, Los Angeles, San Francisco, and New York. Look through the Yellow Pages in each city for cruise line addresses and phone numbers or consult the book *How To Get a Job with a Cruise Line,* mentioned in Appendix B.

Climbing the Ladder

Assistant cruise directors and other cruise staff can move up the ladder to more supervisory and managerial positions. They need to demonstrate that they have organizational skills and that they can delegate and manage people. They also have to be good at detail work and paperwork.

Sometimes earning a promotion has to do with how much experience you have, how good you are—or who has quit or died. As one assistant cruise director pointed out, "It's a good job and most people, once in, don't want to leave."

FIRSTHAND ACCOUNTS

Beverley Citron, Assistant Cruise Director

Beverley Citron began working on cruise ships at the age of twenty-one as a hairdresser. Realizing she would enjoy being part of the social staff more, she took time off to gain the necessary skills. Her hard work paid off, and she landed her first job as a youth counselor. She also worked as a sports director, then was promoted to assistant cruise director.

"I've wanted to work on a ship since I was five years old. I was influenced by two of my uncles who were in the English Royal Navy. Every time they came ashore they'd show me home movies they'd taken of the blue waters of Australia or Hong Kong. All through my school years it was my goal.

"I started out working as a social director for a holiday resort and my local sailing club in England looking after children, planning and implementing their activities. I studied singing and the guitar, then put together an act with musical arrangements and costumes. I was determined to get a job as a social staff member.

"After all those years of applying, when I finally got that letter in the mail saying 'Beverley, we have selected you to be a youth counselor...we'll be sending you an air ticket...please get your visa sorted out...,' I was literally speechless. That was probably the happiest moment of my life."

CRUISE STAFF DUTIES

"The cruise staff are in charge of all the games, activities, and shore excursions for the passengers. In a way it's similar to being a camp counselor, but for adults. Youth counselors, of course, work with children.

"We make sure the passengers are having fun, and we try to come up with activities and events to capture their interest. We might organize a grandmother's tea or give an origami (paper folding) demonstration or stage a treasure hunt. When in port we might chaperone a group of passengers on a tour. Even between scheduled activities, we constantly interact and socialize with the passengers."

THE UPSIDES AND DOWNSIDES

"Working on a cruise ship is my dream job. Every morning I always looked forward to getting up and starting the day. I'm not an office person, it's very difficult for me to stay at a desk all day. I've got a lot of energy, and it's great for me being able to move about the ship making lots of friends, being busy.

"The people you work with become like a family. Sometimes you have to share a cabin and you become very close. Some people worry that working on a cruise ship would be a little like solitary confinement in a prison, that they wouldn't be allowed off of the ship for weeks at a time. But that is hardly the case. When you arrive in port, you always have an opportunity to go ashore. You can go to the beach, shopping, to nightclubs, discos. There are no days off while you're at sea, but you make up for that when you're in port.

"What I like least is having to watch the clock all day. You have to be on the sports deck by 9:00, down in the lounge by 9:30, getting ready in your cabin to be back up on the deck by 10:00, and so on. You're on a rigid time schedule.

"You have to be constantly energetic and cheerful, even when you don't feel like it. You could work up to fifteen hours a day, but what else are you going to do? The alternative is sitting in your cabin."

ADVICE ON GETTING THAT JOB

"A lot of people give up too easily. They apply once or twice, then get discouraged. I sent my resume out to thirty-six cruise lines every three months. For me it took a couple of years and a lot of patience. And over time, I perfected skills that I could add to my resume. Eventually, it paid off. You have to be persistent."

A TYPICAL DAY

8:00 Get up and have breakfast.

8:30 Go to the sports deck to make sure tapes are set up for aerobics classes.

9:00 Teach the class for thirty minutes.

9:30 Sign up passengers for shuffleboard tournament.

9:45 Supervise tournament.

10:45 Sign up passengers for ring toss.

11:00 Teach passengers how to play ring toss.

11:30 Socialize with passengers.

noon Have lunch break, then do paperwork or take short nap.

2:00 Go to sports deck for informal play, explain rules of various games, and continue to announce upcoming events.

3:00 Go to basketball game.

3:45 Get tapes ready for afternoon aerobics class.

4:00 Teach aerobics.

4:30 Pack up sports deck for the day.

5:00 Get showered and dressed for cocktail party.

5:10 Attend cocktail party.

6:30 Take dinner break.

7:30 Get ready for evening Bingo game.

8:00 Supervise Bingo game.

10:00 Attend dancing under the stars.

12:00 Supervise midnight buffet.

WHAT MADE IT ALL WORTHWHILE

"Years ago, when I started as a youth counselor, there was a little ten-year-old boy who came on the ship with his parents maybe twice a year for three years. He stayed by my side the whole time, always interested, always asking if he could help. When I was off duty, he'd beg his mother to take him to meet me for tea.

"The years went by and I lost touch with him. Later, when I was working in a school to train cruise personnel, one of the other teachers took a group of trainees on a tour of a ship. She met one of the ship's assistant cruise directors and asked him to show her trainees around. After the tour, the floor was opened to questions. Someone wanted to know how he had gotten involved with this kind of work.

"He told them how he had started going on cruises at the age of ten, and that he had been strongly influenced by one lady he'll never forget. 'She got me interested in cruising,' he told the trainees. 'I stuck to her like a stamp to a letter, trying to learn everything I could. I told her that one day I'd be working on a ship, and here I am.'

"The other teacher asked what the lady's name was and he told her—Beverley Citron. She arranged a reunion for us. I felt so good knowing that I had influenced someone like that."

Frank Cassisa, Certified Personal Trainer

Frank Cassisa is a certified personal trainer at a national health and fitness chain.

WHAT THE JOB'S REALLY LIKE

"Fitness instruction is just like computers; it's always changing, and there's always something new coming out. To be the best trainer, you have to stay on top of everything.

"One of the best settings is working in a health club. You don't have to generate business because the business is already there in the club. You also can have a private practice, at your own place or going to people's homes. But once you're outside of a club setting, you're talking totally different insurance coverage. If you work out of your own home or in a client's home you need to cover yourself. You're more open for a lawsuit. At a club you come under their insurance.

"I work for a club and I'm covered by their insurance, but even then it doesn't mean someone couldn't come after me personally. But it would have to be plain stupidity to do something that could cause a client to get hurt. Safety is the key.

"We have to check the equipment before the client actually uses that equipment. You have to be fully aware of the human body and how it should move and shouldn't move. If there are any complications or special populations you're working with, diabetics, for example, or rehab cardiac patients, people with arthritis, or pregnant women, there are different ways to train them.

"When you're a certified personal trainer you not only learn about nutrition and kinesiology—which is the study of the movement of the body, learning how the muscles react to certain exercises—you also learn first aid. All certified personal trainers must be certified in CPR.

"With the general population, people who want to improve their fitness, you first have to take a health history, get the doctor's name and number, and ask the right questions: age, smoking, any history of health risk factors. If we think some people are not ready for a training program, we'll refuse them and have them contact their doctor for a physical.

"The perfect scenario for someone not ready is the forty-five-year-old male who smokes, is overweight, and has somebody in his family with diabetes. This person could be a walking time bomb. It would be up to the doctor to do a stress test to see if the patient is ready. We don't do any diagnosing. We're not doctors or dietitians; we have to refer people to professionals if we can't answer their questions or if their condition needs medical attention.

"If a client is a go-ahead, we assess him or her and try to get in all the elements of physical fitness such as flexibility, muscular strength and endurance, cardiovascular endurance, and body composition. Normally a training session is an hour. Clients come once or twice a week to meet with the trainer. And they should come on their own the other days."

HOW FRANK GOT STARTED

"For me it's always been my hobby, but now I'm getting paid for it. I studied through ACE and took their two-part exam, a written and a practical. I love to work out and I love to teach people. I work five days a week. When I take my two-hour lunch break I'm working out. You have to be driven and absorb the whole lifestyle."

ADVICE FROM FRANK

"You need a great attitude and you have to practice what you preach. To a client you're a friend, father figure, role model. They'll follow someone who has the results they're looking for.

"Caring is also important. You need a firm hand but diplomatic skills. You're an instructor, not a dictator."

Roberta Updegraff, Church Youth Leader

Roberta Updegraff has been a youth leader with the Lycoming Presbyterian Church in Williamsport, Pennsylvania, since 1990. In addition to her teacher certification for K–12, she has taken courses in Christian education and youth work, including family, child, and adolescent psychology. She also has participated in church sponsored workshops.

HOW ROBERTA GOT STARTED

"Nothing in particular 'drew' me to working with young people— I discovered I liked them! When I graduated from college and began substituting, I ended up in middle school (substitute teacher purgatory). I found I could roll with the punches and throw a few of my own.

"Adolescent antics haven't changed much in twenty-odd years, so I've been able to navigate the pitfalls with a sense of humor. For example, when students sit in the wrong seat, I call them by the other name all day. They think me stupid, and are having so much fun duping me, they don't bother with other pranks. I enjoy the game. One day John was sitting in Amy's seat and I told him I felt sorry for him. I said that facial hair was a definite dating handicap on a girl, but he'd make a darn good-looking guy. That was years ago, and I still call him Amy when I see him at the high-school.

"I believe because I'm happily married, love learning, and love life, I have an infectious spirit that makes me a natural teacher. I'm firm in standing by my convictions and expectations, but I'm fair, too. I make no bones about classroom misbehavior I will not tolerate. I require respect between fellow classmates and in our relationship with each other.

"Students are expected to be responsible 'employees.' This is their job, and they'd better come to class prepared to do it. That means pencil, paper, textbook, and a cooperative spirit. There are no handouts in my class. If you don't have a pencil, borrow one before I take roll, or buy one from me. If you don't bring an assignment or book, you're out. I send unprepared students to their locker, then to the in-school suspension room to do the class work.

"Once I discovered I could coach in a classroom, youth work seemed the natural extension. When I teach in a public school I touch the future—when I teach in a church youth group, I believe I touch eternity.

"I'm a pretty good storyteller, and I seem to be able to make the Bible come alive with illustrations young people identify with. And I bring my love of learning and God to encouraging spiritual growth in young people.

"In a way, I was dragged into youth work by my teenage son and his friends. Our church didn't have a formal youth group, but we had kids! At times, it seemed we were in danger of being over-run with bored adolescents. So one thing led to another, and I've been doing the job ever since.

"What keeps me working with the kids is they want so badly to be listened to; they crave praise and encouragement. And when an adolescent calls you friend, he or she means it."

WHAT THE JOB IS LIKE

"Every Friday after school, between twelve and thirty middle schoolers hang out in our church basement, for what they fondly call FAF (Friday After Four). I give them time to unwind, listening to contemporary religious music and munching out on snacks and soda. Two other volunteers and myself use the time to listen and to get to know the kids better.

"One of the youths is responsible for organizing and leading a game or relay, which we play after a half-hour social time. (I supply them with idea books the week before. This saves me choosing a game they would deem 'totally lame.' They'll go along with the zaniest youth-initiated activities, games they'd refuse to participate in if I chose them.)

"I then coach a half-hour Bible study. We stick to the Gospels, since many of the kids are unchurched school friends. I try not to interject my opinions, but encourage 'kid talk,' backed-up by 'digging into the scriptures.' We have prayer time, where kids break up into covenant groups and pray for one another.

"During the week I attend their school activities and take time to drop them a note on some positive thing I've observed. I send birthday cards or a 'missed you' note. Sunday mornings I lead church school and feel like a sheep dog! It's a chaotic time I personally wish would disappear into extinction. Sunday school, even the sound of it, is scary!

"And kids are not thrilled about rolling out of bed early on Sunday morning to come and do paperwork! I try to make it hands-on, with a lot of drama, simulation, and lively discussion. But if I had my way, we'd have brown-bag Bible study on Saturday or Sunday afternoon instead. But 'this is the way it's always been done.' (At least since Sunday school opened the door for public education over a hundred years ago!)

"I'm a member of the Youth Advisory Board and the Christian Education Committee, and I am expected to submit a youth report, as well as write a youth newsletter.

"This is a part-time job, but it takes a full-time heart. Youth ministry has been a job that stretches, frustrates, and most of all transforms me. I have learned to be a better listener to my own children by experiencing the loneliness of many of these kids. I don't take my children's mood swings so personally. (An adolescent boy has more hormones pumping through his body every day than a woman in the throes of PMS—hence I say they have AHS, or Adolescent Hormone Syndrome.)

"I've learned humility by being embarrassed in about every way possible. I've learned to ski and moderately like MTV. And a human *can* survive a weekend of sleep deprivation. I know enough to hide my underwear at the overnights (notice they're not sleep overs—there's no sleep!) lest I find them frozen solid at the foot of my sleeping bag.

"Imagine spending time in the chrysalis during metamorphosis. That's what I think it's like being a junior high youth leader. They start out fat, greedy, self-centered caterpillars, and through adolescence learn to give, accept, and put others first. They come out round about their sophomore year more confident about themselves and better citizens because they're motivated not by rules, but by virtue.

"There's a lot of buzz about values and moral education, but I think it's religion that gives the internal motive to aspire to a higher calling. It seems to me impossible to teach honesty, citizenship, or compassion with talking about God. That's what makes youth work so important. I believe in walking the talk. Living a life others notice. Doing the 'right thing' just because it's that. The world is in dire need of heroes and heroines, and I believe I've been called to help young people build character, day-by-day, decision-by-decision, so when the chips are down, this character shines for all the world to notice and benefit from.

"Every other year we take our church youth on a summer-servant experience to Appalachia, where we repair a home for a disadvantaged family or elderly person. The kids do the work. Important jobs like rebuilding steps, caulking windows, tarring a roof, even though at home they've been asked to do little more than take the garbage out.

"I have seen fifty snapshots of caulked windows and repaired screen doors from dozens of different cameras, and I've come to understand how life-changing mission work can be for young people.

"When one rather materialistic and obnoxious fifteen-year-old brought his Gameboy along, despite the fact it was forbidden, he learned a lesson he'll carry with him his whole life. There were two little boys living with their grandmother and a single mom in the house we were working on. These guys had no toys and they slept on a dirty mattress on the floor. This family lived in material poverty, but what shocked this boy the most was the emotional poverty—the biting put-downs, yelling, hitting—things he himself had never experienced.

"Late in the week, this teen let the older boy hold the Gameboy, then play with it 'just a little.' (He didn't want to wear out the batteries!) Finally on the last day, he gave it and his bag full of cartridges to the boys. What a precious moment.

"When asked what he learned through the experience, he said, 'I thought I came to West Virginia to build a house. I found out the house rebuilt me.' I cried.

"Even though most of those work camp days, the only spirit I saw was a bar of soap, there were dozens of moments just like that one. And I feel privileged to be used by God in such an important way!"

THE DOWNSIDES

"Now don't think everything is peaches and cream! Parent volunteers cancel at the last minute, leaving me scrambling to get drivers and things covered. Somebody's always upset with me about something: I didn't give them enough notice, or they didn't like the lesson I taught their kid, or why doesn't our church have hundreds of youths involved like the Presbyterian church across town does?

"Kids are always broke and I'm always lending them money they forget to pay back. Guaranteed, wherever we go someone forgets something. We backtracked ten miles when an expensive pair of Umbros 'accidentally' fell out of the church van window. Of course parents were upset we were twenty minutes late getting back to the church.

"They've always got a crisis. Sometimes it's heart-wrenching. It takes a whole lot of energy and commitment to be involved in their lives.

"Church leaders think I can do a hundred extra 'little things,' because they're related to my teaching position. And everybody's got a better way of doing things or an idea I just have to try."

ADVICE FROM ROBERTA

"My advice? Pray, pray, pray! Then roll up your sleeves and work humbly and joyfully. The next generation depends on you!"

Courtney Jackson, Zoo Volunteer

Courtney is a junior in high school and has been a volunteer worker at a metropolitan zoo and aquarium since she was in the third grade. Here is her account:

"At first I helped out at special events, then I worked in the gift shop. The years after that I spent in a puppeteering program and in a teenagers' education program called ZAP! that allows kids to learn and help out in all areas of the zoo, with a focus on public relations.

"I worked as a guide for the temporary dinosaur exhibit and followed that with my first year as a summer/winter day camp counselor.

"Since then I've worked each summer as a counselor. I got interested in the zoo when my mother started volunteering there, and when she began working there and signing me up for things, I just jumped into the swing of everything. I meet so many people in every department, and everyone wants people to help out or be involved, so it's really easy to do a lot of things that are related, but not 'the same.' "

"I can honestly say that it's the most interesting, most exciting, and absolutely the most fulfilling job I've ever had. I spend most of my time with kids and the smaller, trained animals, and an enormous amount of time with just the everyday zoo visitor. That's really the best part—meeting all the people. I have to say, even if one is the zookeeper, a job at the zoo means communication and dedication. It's not a nine-to-five, half-commitment type thing. You really have to love it and love everything about it, because a lot of things can happen, and everyone has to be prepared for anything and everything.

"It's a ton of fun, though. I wear jeans and shorts, but most of the more official people have to wear uniforms.

"I spend the majority of my time in the summer camp, an area of the education department. I work at camp from 8:00 A.M. to 3:00 P.M. I have to get to the zoo early to clean the room, make Kool Aid, set up and make sample crafts, get the name tags, etc. I also spend that time eating breakfast with my co-workers, reading books from the zoo library, running copies, chopping up fruit and veggies, playing with the education animals, even helping out (if absolutely needed) in the gift shop.

"By the time the kids get there, we have to be armed with badges, walkie-talkies, sign-out sheets, Band Aids in our pockets—you know the drill. Everything to be prepared to take twenty-five kids around the zoo for a day.

"Each age group has a classroom where we eat, play, make crafts, watch videos, have animal visitors, and play games. We use them as home bases because we spend most of our time touring the exhibits and the behind-the-scenes areas, and occasionally feeding the animals. After the kids leave, we have to clean up, plan the next day, and we often help each other out in setting up and/or cleaning. It sounds relatively easy and not very stressful, and it is, usually; but we almost always have some kind of emergency situation every day. Remember, we are responsible for twenty-five kids in each group in the zoo, which means that there are about 125 kids in all running around the zoo. That leaves a lot of room for scraped knees, hats dropped in the exhibits, animals getting loose, belongings getting lost, kids getting sick, animals getting scared. You name it, it happens. And those many little things are what the radios are for.

"Another one of my favorite things about the zoo is that you can never get bored with it. Something exciting happens every day, and everyone has to help out in solving the problem. I work in education, a lot of my friends work in membership and security, and my mother works in retail: I've seen us all working on the same problem at once and getting it fixed in record time. It's amazing what can get accomplished at the zoo.

"It's pretty relaxed, when there's not some huge problem going on. People who are visiting are happy; they come to the zoo because they want to be there, and the people who work at the zoo work there because they love and want to work there. Everyone is in a good mood. That means that there's a lot of laughter, a little leeway, and pretty much a healthy atmosphere."

THE UPSIDES AND DOWNSIDES

"Those three things: the optimistic, happy atmosphere; the daily excitement; and the dedication and love that all the workers feel for their jobs are really the best part about working at the zoo. The only bad things are the natural occurrences that could happen anywhere: if an animal dies, everyone's sad about it; if someone or something is sick, everyone cares for it and worries about it.

When the weather's rainy or really, really cold, everyone likes to hide inside, and there aren't many visitors; however, it's fun to watch the animals enjoy any type of unusual weather.

"The best thing about it is the love it creates in everyone. Even if someone has not intended to get so involved, it kind of pulls you into the swing of everything. Seeing animals everyday has made me want to learn about each of them, as a species and as individuals. The same goes for the people. All kinds of people work at the zoo. There's a feeling of community and friendship. I love being there and thinking about it, and just being involved with any zoo function. Once you get into any aspect of the zoo, it's hard to not get involved with everything else, or to get out of it. It's very much a job of passion, for you have to love what you're doing and know how to do it. At the zoo it's not hard to fall in love—fast."

ADVICE FROM COURTNEY

"To someone who wants to get involved with a zoo, I say do it—in any measure, way, shape, or form. Whether the time agent makes it a large part of the schedule or a small part, you should get involved. Also take it easy, don't rush in too much. Every zoo is different for every different person, and it takes a while to get into everything you want to do. Be friendly and make as many friends as you can. That's almost the entire point of working in such a huge and fun environment.

"I honestly think that it's the most fun job a person could have. Everyone learns a lot, and not only may you affect the visitors, but the animals as well. And I have to warn you, they'll affect you, too.

"And I know that no matter where I go when I'm traveling, I'll be able to go to the local zoo and be comfortable around people and animals I know about."

PROFESSIONAL ASSOCIATIONS

Established in 1910, the American Camping Association (ACA) is an organization of camp professionals who are dedicated to enhancing the lives of children and youth through the camping experience. ACA accredits summer camps based on nationally accepted standards for health, safety, and program quality.

The American Camping Association's 5000-plus members cover all areas of the camp profession, including agencies serving youth and adults, independent camps, religious and fraternal organizations, and public and municipal agencies.

ACA membership is represented by camp owners and directors, executives, clergy, business representatives, consultants, camp and organization staff members, volunteers, students, retirees, and other professionals associated with the operation of camps for children and adults.

For information on careers in camping and summer counselor opportunities, contact:

American Camping Association
   5000 State Road 67 North
   Martinsville, IN 46151

For information on careers with the YMCA, contact:

YMCA of the USA
   101 North Wacker Drive
   Chicago, IL 60606

For information on camping jobs and openings contact the following organizations:

4-H Extension Service
   3860 S Building USDA
   Washington, DC 20250-0900

Boys and Girls Clubs of America
   771 First Avenue
   New York, NY 10017

Boy Scouts of America
   1325 Walnut Hill Lane
   P.O. Box 152079
   Irving, TX 75015-2079

Camp Fire Boys and Girls, Inc.
   4601 Madison Avenue
   Kansas City, MO 64110

Christian Camping International
   P.O. Box 646
   Wheaton, IL 60189

Girl Scouts of USA
   420 Fifth Avenue
   New York, NY 10018-2702

Jewish Welfare Board
   15 East Twenty-sixth Street
   New York, NY 10016

For information on water safety courses and first aid and CPR, contact local chapters of the American Red Cross or its national headquarters:

American Red Cross National Headquarters
   Seventeenth & D Streets, NW
   Washington, DC 20006

For information on local government jobs in recreation, contact the nearest department of parks and recreation.

For information on jobs in recreation and parks contact:

National Recreation and Park Association
  Division of Professional Services
  2775 South Quincy Street, Suite 300
  Arlington, VA 22206

For information on careers in employee services and recreation, contact:

The American Association for Leisure and Recreation (AALR)
  1900 Association Drive
  Reston, VA 22091

National Employee Services and Recreation Association
  2211 York Road, Suite 207
  Oakbrook, IL 60521

The National League for Nursing publishes a variety of nursing and nursing education materials, including a list of nursing schools and informatiosn on financial aid. For a complete list of NLN publications, write to them for a career information brochure.

National League for Nursing (NLN)
  Communications Department
  350 Hudson Street
  New York, NY 10014

For a list of B.S.N. and graduate programs, write to:

American Association for Colleges of Nursing
  1 Dupont Circle, Suite 503
  Washington, DC 20036

Information on career opportunities as a registered nurse is available from:

American Nurses Association
  600 Maryland Avenue SW, Suite 100 West
  Washington, DC 20024-2571

Most professional associations have prepared pamphlets and information packets including up-to-date salary figures, education requirements, and job outlooks. Write to any of the following specialty organizations for their material.

The American Organization of Nurse Executives
840 North Lake Shore Drive
Chicago, IL 60611

National Nursing Staff Development Organization
437 Twin Bay Drive
Pensacola, FL 32534

General information about emergency medical technicians and paramedics is available from:

National Association of Emergency Medical Technicians
9140 Ward Parkway
Kansas City, MO 64114

Information concerning training courses, registration, and job opportunities can be obtained by writing to the State Emergency Medical Service Director, listed in your phone book.

High schools often offer a health occupations program that will allow students to get a taste of all the different medical paths. Students in this program take medical skills classes in the tenth grade. In the eleventh or twelfth grade they spend thirty-six weeks studying medical courses, going on field trips to hospitals and community centers, and riding with ambulances or fire/rescue trucks. By the time they finish, they will know if being a paramedic or a doctor or an emergency room nurse would be the career they'd prefer.

This program is open to all students dedicated to pursuing a career in health occupations. Students in this program also must be members of HOSA—Health Occupations Students of America.

For more information contact the high school guidance counselor or health occupations teacher or write to:

Health Occupations Students of America (HOSA)
6309 North O'Connor Road, Suite 215 LB117
Irving, TX 75039-3510

To find out more about working for a cruise line, contact:

Cruise Line International Association
    500 Fifth Avenue, Suite 1407
    New York, NY 10110

For information on recreation/education-related careers in museums contact:

American Association of Museums
    P.O. Box 4002
    Washington, DC 20042-4002

For information on training and certification for a career as a personal trainer, contact the following associations:

American Council on Exercise (ACE)
    P.O. Box 910449
    San Diego, CA 92191

(provides certification for personal trainers)

American College of Sports Medicine (ACSM)
    Member and Chapter Services Department
    P.O. Box 1440
    Indianapolis, IN 46206

Orthopedic Certification Board (ONCB)
    Box 56 East Holly Avenue
    Pitman, NJ 08071

International Physical Fitness Association
    415 West Court Street
    Flint, MI 48503

Information about careers as restaurant and food service managers, food and beverage servers, chefs, cooks, and other kitchen workers, as well as information on how to obtain directories of two- and four-year college programs in restaurant and food service management and shorter courses that will prepare you for other food service careers is available from:

The Educational Foundation of the National Restaurant Association
    250 South Wacker Drive, Suite 1400
    Chicago, IL 60606

Information about certification as a food service management professional is also available from the above address.

General information on hospitality careers may be obtained from:

Council on Hotel, Restaurant, and Institutional Education
1200 Seventeenth Street NW
Washington, DC 20036-3097

For information on the American Culinary Federation's apprenticeship and certification programs for cooks, as well as a list of accredited culinary programs, write to:

American Culinary Federation
P.O. Box 3466
St. Augustine, FL 32085

General information on food and beverage service jobs is available from:

The Educational Foundation of the National Restaurant Association
250 South Wacker Drive, Suite 1400
Chicago, IL 60606

APPENDIX B

RECOMMENDED READING

Some chapters of the American Camping Association publish free directories, sponsor camp fairs, and provide referral services listing ACA-accredited camps in their region. Call the ACA office nearest you.

The Guide to ACA Accredited Camps, 1997–98 edition, lists locations, programs, and costs for more than 2,000 ACA-accredited day and resident camps from coast to coast. The guide also provides helpful specialty indexes plus information on how to tell when a child is ready for camp, how to choose a camp, questions to ask a camp director, and how to pack for camp.

In addition to its use for pinpointing camps for prospective campers, the guide can be helpful in identifying camps to contact for work possibilities.

It is available for $16.95 and can be ordered by calling 800–428–CAMP.

Peterson's Summer Opportunities for Kids and Teenagers is an in-depth resource offering information on 1,400 camps and other summer programs. Available for $28.95 (including shipping and handling), it can be ordered by calling the ACA Bookstore at 800–428–CAMP or Peterson's at 800–338–3282, ext. 600.

Bookstore
    American Camping Association
        5000 State Road 67 North
        Martinsville, IN 46151-7902
        800–428–CAMP
        E-mail: bookstore@aca-camps.org

Ordering information for materials describing careers and academic programs in recreation is available from:

National Recreation and Park Association
    Division of Professional Services
    2775 South Quincy Street, Suite 300
    Arlington, VA 22206

The American Association for Leisure and Recreation publishes information sheets on twenty-five separate careers in parks and recreation. For price and ordering information, contact:

AALR
    1900 Association Drive
    Reston, VA 22091

How To Get a Job with a Cruise Line (by Mary Fallon Miller, Ticket to Adventure Publishing, P.O. Box 41005, St. Petersburg, FL 33743-1005, 800–929–7447) includes descriptions of all the various jobs, an inside look at the different cruise lines, interviews with cruise personnel, and valuable tips on how to go about getting a job.

Opportunities in Museums and *Opportunities in Zoos and Aquariums* (both by Blythe Camenson, published by NTC Contemporary Publishing) provide information for work experiences related to educational recreation.

For those interested in camp or institutional cooking as a career, *Food for Fifty* (by Grace Shugart and Mary Molt, Macmillan Publishing Co., New York) is a must.